BLACK AMBASSADORS

Everyday a Diplomatic Legacy

Dr. Carlton McLellan

BK Royston Publishing
Jeffersonville, IN
http://www.bkroystonpublishing.com
bkroystonpublishing@gmail.com

ISBN: 978-1-967282-89-0
Ebook ISBN: 978-1-967282-90-6

LCCN: 2026900869

Printed in the United States of America

Acknowledgements and Dedications

This book would not have been possible without the support and contributions of so many people over the many years I have engaged in research focused on the history and contributions of Black American U.S. Ambassadors. I can't acknowledge or thank everyone, but there are a few that I must thank by name, and to whom I dedicated this book.

Most importantly, to the main women in my life, my mother Jean Springer, my wife Dr. Venitha Pillay, and my two lovely stepdaughters, Kiara Soobrayan and Tahlia Soobrayan, thank you for your love and support, and for listening to me on countless occasions as I talked about Black Ambassadors or after I finished an interview with one of them and needed someone to share my excitement.

To the late Ambassador Edward Dudley who will always be known as "The First" and who blazed the path for Black Americans to not only become Ambassadors, but also to lead America's diplomatic efforts in posts and portfolios all over the world, outside of the so-called "Negro Circuit".

To the late Ambassador Ronald Palmer who was among the first Black Ambassadors I had the privilege of interviewing and spending numerous hours with, learning about his life, career, and history.

To the late Ambassador Edward Perkins who, as President of the Association of Black American Ambassadors (ABAA), saw the value in my work and brought me onboard as a Senior Fellow with ABAA.

To the late Ambassador Ruth Davis, who renewed my Senior Fellowship with ABAA as she took over as its President. Ambassador Davis also gave me so much of her time to just talk and share our mutual passion for telling the story of the history and contributions of Black leadership in diplomacy and international affairs. I feel privileged to have spent time with her at her home just a couple of weeks prior to her passing.

To the late Ambassador Steve McGann, with whom I had countless conversations about the future of the Association of Black American Ambassadors (ABAA) as he assumed his presidency of the association. We did not get to do all the amazing things we discussed, but his leadership and council helped me push my own personal research on this topic forward.

To Ambassador Charles Ray for allowing me to share writing space with him as we jointly write together (at the time of my publishing of this book) and for his prolific writing that inspires me and so many others to put pen to paper.

To all of the Black Ambassadors past and present, who are the subject of this book. I dedicate this to you, to your years of service, to your leadership, and to your roles in Black and American history.

Finally, to everyone who, over the years, has played even a small part in helping gather data, review transcripts, conduct online research, comb through speeches, or just talk with me about my passion for studying these Black American leaders.

Dr. Carlton McLellan (Author, Black Ambassadors)

TABLE OF CONTENTS

Foreword

The United States appointed its first Ambassador in 1893, when Thomas F. Bayard was named Ambassador to Great Britain and the Court of St. James on March 30. Since then, approximately 3,500 people have been appointed to this, the highest diplomatic post a nation can hold. Of that number, only 166, or 4.7 percent, were Black at the time of writing. Before the end of the slave trade in 1808, people of African descent made up 20 percent of the US population, but after that, it declined and has been as low as 10 percent. The current percentage is around 12 percent. At no time, however, has the percentage of African Americans appointed to the office of Ambassador been even remotely close to the lowest percentage of the greater population. It is, nevertheless, important to celebrate the contributions of Black Americans who have led America's diplomatic missions worldwide as its Ambassadors.

Though few in number, Black Ambassadors have played an outsized role in communicating American values to countries and in adding credence to this country as a beacon of human rights and the dignity of every individual. As one of this select few who have had the privilege to serve this country as chief of a diplomatic mission, with the title and rank of Ambassador, on two occasions, I can attest that it was people like Ambassador Terence Todman, Ambassador Ruth Davis, and Ambassador Edward Perkins who inspired me to believe that it was even possible for a farm boy from East Texas to hold such a high office. But, it was not just young African Americans that they inspired. They also demonstrated to every American that, regardless of race or ethnicity, we all have something to contribute when given the opportunity, and to the world that there is strength in diverse societies.

During the Cold War, when the state of race relations in the United States was a strong point in Soviet propaganda, especially in the newly independent countries of Africa and

Asia, Black diplomats, and especially Black Ambassadors, were a strong counterargument.

In the current climate, when there is a rising tide of nativism and opposition to diversity, equity, and inclusion—even in the United States —it is critical that the public have access to an argument for inclusion and the advantages it brings to society. Such an argument is strengthened by telling and acknowledging the stories of Black Americans who have led the nation's diplomatic engagements as U.S. Ambassadors.

In my opinion, no one is better equipped to do that than Dr. Carlton McLellan, who has assembled the most extensive database of information on Black American Ambassadors. This introductory volume offers glimpses into their individual and collective lives, contributions, and accomplishments. It is the result of 20 years of dedicated study and research, and will serve as an outstanding introduction to Black leadership in foreign affairs and as encouragement for younger generations to aspire to such heights. The book is written in an accessible, straightforward timeline format that provides daily inspiration by showcasing moments in American history through the lens of these Black American leaders.

Charles A. Ray, Former ambassador to Cambodia (2002-2005) and Zimbabwe (2009-2012), and Deputy Assistant Secretary of Defense for POW/Missing Personnel Affairs (2006-2009)

Introduction

Each year, Black History Month is celebrated during the month of February, but Black History has and continues to be made every single day of the calendar year. In virtually all areas of society and life, from the arts to business to justice and law to politics to sports, to entertainment, and beyond, one can find fascinating milestones, key moments, and interesting contributions that have been led by or involving Black Americans. The pages that follow focus on an often underappreciated and underexposed area of Black History and leadership– foreign affairs and diplomacy. Specifically, the rank and position of Ambassador is the diplomatic leadership role used to illustrate the contributions of Black Americans to U.S. and foreign affairs and diplomacy.

Black American U.S. Ambassadors have had formal leadership roles that have translated into their service as vanguards of American diplomacy. They have forged new pathways where few Black Americans have been able to do so while also laying the groundwork for an increased Black presence in American and foreign affairs. Through their vision and leadership, Black Ambassadors have introduced fresh ideas, advanced innovative policies, and pushed for change that has reshaped American and global policy and relations. Their experiences and work have not only opened doors for greater participation by Black Americans but also demonstrate how diplomacy can be a force for domestic and global progress and mutual understanding.

Black Americans have led and made significant contributions to U.S. foreign and diplomatic relations since the mid-19th century. Heinl (1973) argues that America's first Black diplomat was Ebenezer Don Carlos Basset whom President Ulysses S. Grant appointed as Minister to Haiti in 1869. In contrast, Ambassador Horace Dawson, Jr. argued that it was actually William Alexander Leidesdorff who was America's first Black diplomat when he was appointed, during the presidency of James Polk, as Vice Consul in Yerba Buena, Mexico (today's San Francisco) in October of 1845 (Dawson 1993). As I have argued elsewhere (McLellan 2015), perhaps the difference in the interpretations of "diplomat" in these two arguments stems from the sources of the appointments, as Mr. Basset was appointed by a U.S. president, whereas Mr. Leidersdorff's appointment was recommended by Tomas O. Larkin, the U.S. Consul in Monterey, Mexico, during the Polk administration. Regardless of the accepted argument, this shows that Black Americans have led in diplomacy and international affairs as far back as the late 19th century. This early leadership of U.S. diplomacy was early on, in the form of consuls, envoys, or ministers. It was only in 1893, when the U.S. first began elevating its diplomatic leadership roles to that of an Ambassador, as its highest title and rank.

The responsibility of an American Ambassador includes serving as the U.S. President's official representative in the place of service – whether a foreign nation, an international organization, or key foreign affairs issues–and protecting the health, welfare, and interests of all Americans under their responsibility. These Ambassadors are appointed by the U.S. President and confirmed by the U.S. Senate. This is the professional role of leadership that this book is concerned with.

Since 1893, when the U.S. first began using the title and rank of Ambassador for its chief diplomatic representative abroad, there have been approximately **3,500 American Ambassadors**. **Only 166** of those have been Black (at the time of writing). This means that less than 5% of America's Ambassadors who have held this distinguished title, rank, and responsibility have been Black Americans. This is an unfortunate and quite frankly shameful fact, but at the same time, it also means that more should be known about this small percentage of our Black American diplomatic leaders, and we must educate about and celebrate their lives and careers. It is incumbent upon those of us concerned with Black history to unpack their stories for inspirational, historical, and educational values. This is a central goal of this present writing.

This book focuses on Black American U.S. Ambassadors, is important and relevant for multiple reasons. First, it helps highlight the contributions of individual Black Americans (and the collective) who have represented and led the United States on the global stage, often breaking racial barriers and challenging and overcoming discrimination. These Ambassadors have played vital roles in diplomacy, international and domestic affairs, and policy-making, shaping how the U.S. is perceived globally. Second, understanding their lives, experiences, and history provides insight into the broader struggle for racial justice and equality that Black Americans have faced. Many Black American Ambassadors overcame systemic obstacles to reach their positions, making their stories a testament to perseverance and excellence. Their journeys reflect the progress made in American society while also underscoring the work still needed to achieve equity that is embedded in American ideals.

Thirdly, studying these Ambassadors offers valuable lessons in leadership, negotiation, and cultural diplomacy that can be beneficial to future generations. Their experiences navigating complex domestic and international issues demonstrate how diplomacy can foster peace and cooperation, inspiring future generations to pursue careers in international service, or at the very least, understand the international dimensions of their own chosen career fields. Finally, recognizing Black American Ambassadors ensures that their contributions are not overlooked in historical narratives, particularly those related to Black History and American History at large. By learning about their achievements, we promote a more accurate account of American history, celebrating the Black voices and efforts that have helped shape the nation's domestic and global diplomatic legacy.

The book is formatted as a timeline that includes at least one significant moment in history, each day of the year, involving a Black Ambassador. It covers 365+1 day (including Leap Year), beginning with January 1 and ending with December 31, over a 133-year period. The earliest year covered in these milestones occurs in 1891 with the birth of Jessie Locker (the 2nd Black American to ever be appointed and serve as a U.S. Ambassador), and the latest moment occurs in 2024 (at the time of this original writing). By using this timeline format, the book hopes to drive home the fact that Black History in an area often overlooked and/or where it is claimed that Black voices have been muted – diplomacy and international relations – is made every day. It also demonstrates how Black Americans have and continue to play vital leadership roles in American and global diplomatic relations, and other important professional, social, and economic areas where the Ambassadors highlighted have contributed.

This 365-day timeline of Black U.S. Ambassador moments found in this book, includes birthdays; days of passing (deaths); days of nomination by Presidents as U.S. Ambassadors; Senate confirmation days; days of credential presentations; days of significant speeches; days of significant diplomatic or professional activities; days of book or other publications; days of media coverage; days of termination of ambassadorships; and other key moments in the lives of the Ambassadors covered.

CHAPTER 1:

Black American U.S. Ambassadors: A Small, Mighty, and Diverse Group of Leaders

Despite the small number of Black Americans who have served as U.S. Ambassadors, I have collected, organized, and analyzed a deep amount of data, moments, and achievements that I have begun to unpack to demonstrate their significance to Black history and American and global history. Although this book is not intended to delve deeply into that data and history (other works I have and will continue to release do so), some key data points can help lay a foundation that supports the argument that these individuals do represent a Black diplomatic vanguard. In doing so, the reader will see that these Black Americans have led the way in driving U.S. foreign policy across the world, and, at the same time, they have laid important trails for one another and future Black diplomatic leaders. Additionally, these Black leaders represent the cultural, educational, geographic, and professional diversity and achievements of Black America at large. What follows here is a summative view of some relevant data points concerning the 166 Black Americans who have served as U.S. Ambassadors. These datapoints are current as of the release of this book, but the data may have shifted by the time these words reach various readers after publication.

Of the 166 Black American U.S. Ambassadors, 66% of them (or 109) were still living at the time of publication. Fifty-seven (57) or 34% of them have passed on. Fifty-nine (59) have been women, which means 36%, while 107, or 64%, of them have been male. Between these women and men, 94, or

57%, have been professional diplomats also known as Foreign Service Officers (FSOs). The other 72, or 43%, are what are known as Non-Career Appointees (NCA). As NCAs, they entered their ambassadorial appointments coming from professions outside of the U.S. government's Foreign Service. The main U.S. Foreign Service agency is the U.S. Department of State; however, other agencies also have or had a Foreign Service. This included the U.S. Department of Agriculture (USDA), the U.S. Department of Commerce, the U.S. Agency for International Development (USAID), and the U.S. Information Agency (USIA). The latter two agencies – USAID and USIA – are now officially part of the U.S. Department of State.

Despite whether they were FSO or NCA ambassadorial appointments, Presidents from both major political parties – Democrat and Republican – have appointed Black Americans as U.S. Ambassadors during the nation's history. In 1949, Harry Truman was the first President to appoint a Black Ambassador. In that year, he appointed Edward R. Dudley as U.S. Ambassador to Liberia, making Dudley the first ever Black American to officially hold the presidentially appointed and Senate confirmed title and rank of U.S. Ambassador. Since this appointment, every U.S. President after Truman has appointed at least one Black American as a U.S. Ambassador. In total, a Black American has been appointed as a U.S. Ambassador at least 232 times in the nation's history. At least 66 of the 166 Black American U.S. Ambassadors have been appointed and confirmed successfully to serve more than one ambassadorial tenure during her/his career, which accounts for the total number of times (232) these appointments have occurred successfully.

Overall, Presidents in the Democratic Party have successfully appointed a Black American 130 times as a U.S. Ambassador while their Republic Party counterparts have appointed a Black American on 102 occasions. As the table below shows, following President Truman's initial appointment of Edward Dudley as the first Black American U.S. Ambassador, most of his successors – with the exceptions of Ford and Trump – would appoint a Black American on a progressively higher number of occasions than their predecessor. The presidential trio of Bill Clinton, George W. Bush, and Barack Obama appointed the highest numbers on 40, 45, and 46 occasions, respectively. Unfortunately, after significant gains in the appointment of Black American U.S. Ambassadors from the early 1980s forward, beginning in 2017 with the first term presidency of Donald Trump, there was a significant reversal in the upward trend as he only appointed five (5) Black Americans as his Ambassadors during that first term.

TABLE 1: APPOINTMENT OF BLACK AMERICANS TO THE AMBASSADORSHIP BY U.S. PRESIDENTS*			
President	**Years in Office**	**Political Party**	**# of times each U.S. President appointed a Black Ambassador**
Truman	1945-53	Democrat	1
Eisenhower	1953-61	Republican	3
Kennedy	1961-63	Democrat	3
Johnson	1963-69	Democrat	8
Nixon	1969-74	Republican	11
Ford	1974-77	Republican	5
Carter	1977-81	Democrat	16
Reagan	1981-89	Republican	17
G.H. Bush	1989-93	Republican	17
Clinton	1993-2001	Democrat	40
G.W. Bush	2001-09	Republican	45
Obama	2009-2017	Democrat	46
Trump	2017-2021	Republican	5
Biden	2021-2025	Democrat	15
Trump	2025-Present	Republican	0
TOTAL			**232**

***These numbers have been adjusted and updated since a 2015 publication by the author**

As I have outlined elsewhere (McLellan 2015), there are typically two classifications for an American Ambassador: an Ambassador-in-Residence, responsible for a particular U.S. mission or international organization, and an Ambassador-at-Large, responsible for a particular foreign policy or related portfolio. While the latter is not assigned to a specific country, foreign government, or sovereign she/he is given the responsibility by the American President, for the execution of foreign policy issues of key importance to the United States. According to on-line State Department Office of Historian records, supplemented by reviews of the American Foreign Service Associations (AFSA) website and other available sources, there have been approximately 3,344 different individual Americans who have been appointed and served as Ambassador (In-Residence) to other countries or international institutions, and 56 who have served as a U.S. Ambassador-at-Large or in another capacity with rank of Ambassador (e.g. Ronald Kirk was appointed by President Obama in 2008 as U.S. Trade Representative with Rank of Ambassador). Some have held both ranks during their careers. In total, there have been approximately 3,500 individual U.S.

Ambassadors overall, of which, as has already been stated, only 166 have been Black. The full list is available in the Index.

What the full list of 166 Black Ambassadors does not show is the diversity within this small but important group of leaders. This diversity includes (but is not limited to) their places of birth, higher education attainment, professions, places of ambassadorial appointment, memberships in professional/social organizations, and even collegiate, amateur, and/or professional athletics.

Places of Birth. Black Americans who would go on to become U.S. Ambassadors were born in at least 28 different U.S. states and the District of Columbia (Washington, DC), as well as at least 10 different countries. New York state was the birthplace of the most (20), while Louisiana (11) and Virginia (11) are a close second, and Illinois (10) and the District of Columbia (Washington, DC) (10) share the third place. Other notable states that were the birthplace of Black Americans who would eventually become U.S. Ambassadors include North Carolina (9) and my birth state of Ohio (7).

Globally, four (4) were born on the African continent – Ambassador Patrick Gaspard and Ambassador Tulinabo Mushingi (both born in Zaire, now called the Democratic Republic of Congo; Ambassador Daniel Yohannes was born in Addis Ababa, Ethiopia, and Ambassador John Nkengasong was born in Cameroon. Two were born on the European continent, specifically in Germany– Ambassador Lesslie Alexander (Frankfurt) and Ambassador Brian Nichols (Berlin).

Ten were born in the Caribbean, including the following:

TABLE 2: TEN BLACK AMERICAN AMBASSADORS BORN IN THE CARIBBEAN		
Name	**Island or City**	**Country**
Elliott Percival Skinner	Port of Spain	Trinidad & Tobago
Terence A. Todman	St. Thomas	U.S. Virgin Islands
Melvin H. Evans	St. Croix	U.S. Virgin Islands
Vernelle Trim FitzPatrick	St. Croix	U.S. Virgin Islands
Betty Eileen King	Kingstown	St. Vincent & The Grenadines
Roy Leslie Austin	Kingstown	St. Vincent & The Grenadines
Roland Wentworth Bullen	Carriacou	Grenada
John Estrada	Laventille	Trinidad & Tobago
Nicholas "Nick" Perry	Saint Andrew Parish	Jamaica
Joel Danies	Jacmel	Haiti

Higher Education. Educationally, the 166 received earned academic degrees from a range of universities both in the United States and abroad. Forty-one (41) Black Americans who would become U.S. Ambassadors received at least one of their degrees from a Historically Black College & University (HBCU) such as Hampton University, Howard University, Johnson C. Smith College, Lincoln University, Spelman College, or others. At least 52 of the 166 received at least one of their degrees from an Ivy League higher education institution such as Cornell University, Dartmouth College, Harvard University, University of Pennsylvania, Stanford University, or others. At least seven (7) of the 166 earned at least one of their higher education degrees from an international institution such as the Institut Supérieur Pedagogique in the Democratic Republic of Congo, Oxford University in England, the University of Windsor in Canada, or others. Finally, several of the Ambassadors also received degrees from military universities such as the Naval Academy, U.S. Naval War College, Army War College, National Defense University, and Industrial College of the Armed Forces, among others.

Professions. As previously indicated, at least 72 of the Black American Ambassadors came from a profession outside of the official U.S. diplomatic establishment (Foreign Service). These NCAs represented professionals that include attorneys, banking and finance, clergy or religious leadership, civil rights advocates, community organizing, education and scholarship, entertainment, general business, journalism and media, international development and/or humanitarian service, law enforcement, military officers and service personnel, politics or public service, security, telecommunications, and more. The importance of this diversity of professions is in its demonstration that no matter one's specific, chosen career path, achievement and excelling in that professional area does provide leadership skills that can be recognized by the U.S. President as needed to oversee America's global interests. This is a lesson I would especially hope young people considering any career would take note of and recognize.

Places of ambassadorial appointment. In overseeing American foreign affairs interests worldwide, these 166 Black Americans have done so in over 200 countries as well as to global agencies such as the United Nations, regional bodies such as the European Union, and over global policy issues such as counter-terrorism. Liberia has been the nation that has hosted the most Black American Ambassadors (on 8 occasions), and overall, Sub-Saharan Africa is the region that has seen the most Black American Ambassadorial postings (155 occasions).

Professional/Social Organizations: Membership in Divine Nine. At least 34 of the 166 Black American U.S. Ambassadors are members of the nine Black Greek letter organizations referred to as The Divine Nine. Although the following table does not claim to be exhaustive, it lists those Black Greek letter organizations (fraternities and sororities) to which Black American U.S. Ambassadors belong.

TABLE 3: DIVINE NINE MEMBERSHIP OF BLACK AMBASSADORS

Fraternity or Sorority	Members
Kappa Alpha Psi, Fraternity, Inc. (5)	Jessie D. Locker Richard L. Jones Ronald DeWayne Palmer Edward J. Perkins Carl B. Stokes
Alpha Phi Alpha, Fraternity, Inc. (9)	Samuel Clifford Adams Orison Rudolph Aggrey Walter Charles Carrington Horace Dawson George W. B. Haley Donald McHenry Gerald E. Thomas Terence A. Todman Barry L. Wells

Omega Psi Phi, Fraternity, Inc. (8)	Maurice D. Bean Jerome Gary Cooper Jerome Holland Carl T. Rowan Joseph M. Segars Charles R. Stith Gentry O. Smith Teddy B. Taylor
Phi Beta Sigma, Fraternity, Inc. (1)	Harry K. Thomas, Jr. (Honorary)
Iota Phi Theta, Fraternity, Inc. (0)	None known
Alpha Kappa Alpha, Sorority, Inc. (3)	Gayleatha B. Brown Mattie R. Sharpless Diane E. Watson
Delta Sigma Theta, Sorority, Inc. (8)	Shirley Elizabeth Barnes Carol Moseley Braun Pamela Bridgewater Harriet L. Elam-Thomas Patricia Roberts Harris Anne Forrester Holloway June Carter Perry Barbara Mae Watson
Zeta Phi Beta, Sorority, Inc. (0)	None known
Sigma Gamma Rho, Sorority, Inc. (0)	None known

Updated from: McLellan (2015).

The bonds of brotherhood and sisterhood found within the individual member organizations of the Divine Nine, as well as across them, are intended to be a lifelong commitment to positive values and service at the very least. The individuals who would become U.S. Ambassadors made this commitment at some point during their lives (whether as undergraduate students, graduate students, or working professionals) to these same principles and values through their joining of one of these organizations. Such commitment is also a mark of a diplomatic leader, and among the many positive characteristics that would inevitably be a part of one's selection to lead U.S. diplomatic and foreign affairs as an Ambassador.

There are other comparative datapoints I could cover, including how many of these Black American Ambassadors held doctoral degrees; how many were participants in international youth or volunteer programs such as Operation Crossroads Africa; how many served in the U.S. Peace Corps; how many were college, Olympic, and/or professional athletes, and more. However, if I include everything in this one text, I would never get to the 365-day timeline of milestones, firsts, and unsung moments that is the book's purpose. Therefore, I will save future in-depth explorations of the comparative data points of Black American Ambassadors for another time and proceed to a month-by-month, day-by-day, celebration of the 166 Black Americans who have held the nation's highest diplomatic title and rank – Ambassador.

As one progresses through this book, there should be a recognition that the 166 Black American Ambassadors represent a remarkable range of backgrounds, accomplishments, and experiences. At the same time, their stories intersect in meaningful ways—both with one another and with the lives and work of individuals who may not have formally held the title of Ambassador but whose paths connect with this broader history of leadership and diplomacy.

In other words, there are mutual lines of intersection among and between the 166 Black Ambassadors, as well as lines of intersection between them and others who may not have held the leadership role of Ambassador.

As such, for those seeking to understand leadership and perhaps looking for even the smallest commonalities they may have with global leaders, some of the datapoints about Black American U.S. Ambassadors described above (or further throughout this book), may be of relevance.

CHAPTER 2:
JANUARY

January 1

1961 On this day in 1961, Jendayi E. Frazer was born in the state of Virginia. Frazer was a university educator, scholar, and diplomat who would serve as U.S. Ambassador to South Africa from 2004 to 2005.

1979 On this day in 1979, Ambassador William Beverly Carter departed to take up the leadership post as U.S. Ambassador to Liberia. Carter was a journalist and career diplomat who served as a U.S. Ambassador on three separate occasions: to Tanzania (1972 to 1975), to Liberia (1976 to 1979), and at-Large as Liaison with State and Local Government (1979 to 1981).

1982 On this day in 1982, Ambassador Melvin Evans presented his credentials to the leadership in Trinidad and Tobago, officially beginning his tenure in-residence as the leader of the U.S. Mission in the country. Born in the U.S. Virgin Islands, Evans was a medical doctor, public servant, and diplomat who served as U.S. Ambassador to Trinidad and Tobago from 1981 to 1984.

January 2

2009 On this day in 2009, Ambassador June Carter Perry departed from her post as leader of the U.S. Mission in Sierra Leone. Perry was a career diplomat who served as U.S. Ambassador to Lesotho from 2004 to 2007 and to Sierra Leone from 2007 to 2009.

January 3

1975 On this day in 1975, Ambassador Terence Todman departed from his post as leader of the U.S. Mission in Guinea. Born in the U.S. Virgin Islands, Todman was a military veteran and career diplomat. He had the distinction of being a U.S. Ambassador, on six separate occasions, more than any other Black American in history. Todman served as U.S. Ambassador to: Chad from 1969 to 1972; Guinea from 1972 to 1975; Costa Rica from 1974 to 1977; Spain from 1978 to 1983; Denmark from 1983 to 1989; and, Argentina from 1989 to 1993.

January 4

2003 On this day in 2003, Ambassador Charles Ray presented his credentials to the leadership in Cambodia, officially beginning his tenure in-residence as the leader of the U.S. Mission in this East Asian nation. Ambassador Ray would serve in this leadership role until 2005. Ray was a military veteran and career diplomat who served as U.S. Ambassador to Cambodia from 2002 to 2005 and then to Zimbabwe from 2009 to 2012.

January 5

1980 On this day in 1980, Ambassador Anne Forrester Holloway presented her credentials to the leadership in Mail, officially beginning her tenure in-residence, as leader of the U.S. Mission in that country. Forrester Holloway was a scholar, activist, university educator, and diplomat who served as U.S. Ambassador to Mali from 1979 to 1981.

January 6

2021 On this day in 2021, Ambassador Natalie E. Brown released a statement to the Ugandan community where she served as U.S. Ambassador, condemning the events that occurred at the U.S. Capitol building. On that day, at the behest of outgoing U.S. President Donald Trump, who continued to question the results of the election that saw his defeat, armed rioters stormed the Capitol Building, shocking all who watched. In her statement, Ambassador Brown reiterated America's commitment to human rights and democracy and reassured the Ugandan people that, although the U.S. is not perfect, it continues to value democracy, freedom of speech, and human rights for all.

Brown was a career diplomat who, at the time of this writing, was serving as U.S. Ambassador to Uganda.

January 7

1974 On this day in 1974, Ambassador O. Rudolph Aggrey presented his credentials to the leadership of Senegal, officially beginning his tenure in-residence as leader of the U.S. Mission to that West African nation. He would also simultaneously serve as U.S. Ambassador to The Gambia until 1977. He would later also serve as U.S. Ambassador to Romania from 1977 to 1981. Ambassador Aggrey was a career diplomat and university educator.

January 8

1989 On this day in 1998, Ambassador Terence Todman departed from his post as leader of the U.S. Mission in Denmark. Todman was a military veteran and career diplomat who has the distinction of being a U.S. Ambassador more than any other Black American in history (six total), including: to Chad (1969-1972), to Guinea (1972-1975), to Costa Rica (1974-1977), to Spain (1978-1983), to Denmark (1983-1989), and, to Argentina (1989-1993).

Major Milestone Moment

January 9

On this day in 1916, **Jerome H. Holland** was born in Auburn, New York. Holland was an athlete, sociologist, university leader, businessman, and diplomat who served as U.S. Ambassador to Sweden from 1970 to 1972. Prior to his professional career, Holland became the 1st Black American to play football at the Ivy League's Cornell University, where he played from 1935 to 1939, and was a two-time All American. Later, following his business career and his ambassadorship, he would also become the first Black American to be elected to sit on the Board of the New York Stock Exchange, doing so from 1972 to 1980.

January 10

2019 On this day in 2019, Ambassador Arthur W. Lewis passed away. Ambassador Lewis was a military veteran and diplomat who served as U.S. Ambassador to Sierra Leone from 1983 to 1986.

January 11

1998 On this day in 1988, Ambassador Sidney Williams departed from his post as leader of the U.S. Mission in the Bahamas. Williams was an athlete, public servant, businessman, and diplomat who served as U.S. Ambassador to the Bahamas from 1994 to 1998, making him the first Black American to hold that post.

2016 On this day in 2016, Ambassador Carolyn Alsup presented her credentials to the leadership in The Gambia, officially beginning her tenure in-residence, as U.S. Ambassador to that nation. Alsup was a career diplomat who served as U.S. Ambassador to The Gambia from 2015 to 2016.

January 12

2005 On this day in 2005, Ambassador Bismarck Myrick served as the keynote speaker at the Elizabeth City State University annual assembly in memory of Dr. Martin Luther King, Jr. Ambassador Myrick was a military veteran and career diplomat who served as U.S. Ambassador to Lesotho from 1995 to 1998 and Liberia from 1999 to 2002.

January 13

2021 On this day in 2021, the media outlet *Government Executive* published an online article outlining the Association of Black American Ambassadors (ABAA's) recommendations to the incoming Biden Administration on how to improve diversity and inclusivity at the State Department and U.S. Agency for International Development. The ABAA is a national organization incorporated in the District of Columbia whose purpose is to bring together

African Americans who have been appointed by the President and confirmed by the Senate as Ambassadors of the United States. Their goal is to advance public understanding of diplomacy, to promote diversity within the various government agencies responsible for foreign policy, and to put their knowledge at the service of the national interest.

January 14

2000 On this day in 2000, Ambassador Harriet Elam-Thomas presented her credentials to the leadership in Senegal, officially beginning her tenure in-residence, as leader of the U.S. Mission to this West African nation. Elam-Thomas was a university educator and career diplomat who served as U.S. Ambassador to Senegal and Guinea-Bissau concurrently from 1999 to 2002.

January 15

2010 On this day in 2010, Ambassador Bernadette M. Allen departed from her post as leader of the U.S. Mission in Niger. Allen was a career diplomat who served as U.S. Ambassador to Niger from 2006 to 2010.

January 16

1981 On this day in 1981, Ambassador William Beverly Carter ended his tenure as Liaison with State and Local Governments, where he had been serving with the rank of Ambassador-at-Large since 1979. Carter was a journalist and career diplomat who served as U.S. Ambassador to Tanzania from 1972 to 1975, Liberia from 1976 to 1979, and in this role as Liaison with State and Local Governments, with the rank of Ambassador-at-Large from 1979 to 1981.

Major Milestone Moment

January 17

On this day in 1966, **Ambassador Franklin Williams** presented his credentials to the leadership in Ghana, officially beginning his tenure as leader of the U.S. Mission in that West African nation. Williams was a military veteran, civil rights attorney, and diplomat who served as U.S. Ambassador to Ghana from 1965 to 1968, the first Black American to have held this leadership post in this key African nation. Earlier in his career, Williams served as regional director for the West Coast office of the National Association for the Advancement of Colored People (NAACP). While in that role, he won the first ever judgment in a major case involving school desegregation. He would also, later become California's first ever Black Assistant Attorney General (1959).

January 17

1974 On this day in 1974, Ambassador O. Rudolph Aggrey presented his credentials to the leadership in The Gambia, officially beginning his tenure as leader of the U.S. Mission to this African nation. Aggrey was a career diplomat and university educator who served as U.S. Ambassador to Senegal and The Gambia from 1973 to 1977 and Romania from 1977 to 1981.

2025 On this day in 2025, Ambassador Candace Bond received the Hummingbird Gold Medal in the sphere of Bilateral and Diplomatic Relations from Her Excellency Christine Carla Kangaloo, O.R.T.T., President of Trinidad and Tobago. Ambassador Bond was presented this prestigious recognition for her outstanding contributions to strengthening U.S.-Trinidad and Tobago relations, including advancements in security, energy, trade, and regional stability. The Hummingbird Gold Medal is awarded for exceptional service to the nation, recognizing both citizens and non-citizens who have made significant contributions to Trinidad and Tobago. Ambassador Bond was a businesswoman, former Vice President of Motown Records, and diplomat who served as U.S. Ambassador to Trinidad and Tobago from 2022 to 2025.

January 18

2015 On this day in 2015, Ambassador Frankie Reed departed from her concurrent postings as leader of the U.S. Missions in Fiji, Kiribati, Nauru, Tonga, and Tuvalu. Reed was a journalist, attorney, and career diplomat who served as U.S. Ambassador concurrently to these five Pacific Island nations from 2011 to 2015.

January 19

1957 On this day in 1957, William E. Kennard was born in Los Angeles, California. Kennard was a telecommunications expert, attorney, and diplomat who would serve as U.S.

Representative to the European Union (EU), with the rank of Ambassador, from 2010 to 2013.

Major Milestone Moment

January 20

On this day in 1981, 52 American hostages, seized from the U.S. Embassy in Tehran in November 1979, were finally released. Playing a major role in the negotiations and the lead-up to that release was **Ambassador Ulric Haynes**, who was then serving as U.S. Ambassador to Algeria (1977-1981), the country leading and hosting the negotiations. Earlier Foreign Service career, Haynes was serving as the State Department's Desk Officer for Southwest Africa (current day Namibia). At the time, traveling through Southwest Africa required transit through apartheid South Africa. Initially, upon learning Haynes was Black, the South African government refused to grant the visa. After pressure from President Lyndon Johnson, Haynes' visa to travel to and through South Africa was finally approved, making him among the first Black American diplomats to receive a visa to go to apartheid South Africa.

January 20

2001 On this day in 2001, Ambassador Charles Stith departed from his post as leader of the U.S. Mission in Tanzania. Stith was a minister, university educator, administrator, and diplomat who served as U.S. Ambassador to Tanzania from 1998 to 2001.

2009 On this day in 2009, Ambassador Roy Austin departed from his post as leader of the U.S. Mission in Trinidad and Tobago. Austin was born in St. Vincent and the Grenadines. He would become a university educator, scholar, and diplomat who would serve as U.S. Ambassador to Trinidad and Tobago from 2001 to 2009.

2009 On this day in 2009, Ambassador Eric Bost departed from his post as leader of the U.S. Mission in South Africa. Bost was a public servant and diplomat who served as U.S. Ambassador to South Africa from 2006 to 2009.

1990 On this day in 1990, Ambassador Ruth Washington tragically passed in a car accident near her home in Hartsdale, New York, before being able to physically take up her post as U.S. Ambassador to The Gambia. Washington had been appointed by President George H. Bush in 1989 and confirmed by the U.S. Senate that same year as U.S. Ambassador to The Gambia. She was an attorney, university educator, and diplomat, and this would have been her first ambassadorial appointment.

January 21

2000 On this day in 2000, Ambassador Delano Lewis departed from his post as leader of the U.S. Mission in South Africa. Lewis was an attorney, businessman, and diplomat who served as U.S. Ambassador to South Africa from 1999 to 2001.

January 22

1967 On this day in 1967, Ambassador Patricia Roberts Harris officially ended her tenure as U.S Ambassador to Luxembourg, where she had served since 1965. In addition to being the first Black American female to serve as U.S. Ambassador, Harris served as U.S. Secretary of Housing and Urban Development (1977), making her the first Black American woman to ever hold a Cabinet-level post, and the first to ever be part of the Presidential Line of Succession.

January 23

2009 On this day in 2009, President Barack Obama nominated Susan Rice to be Permanent Representative of the U.S. to the United Nations (UN) with the rank of Ambassador. Following Senate confirmation, Ambassador Rice would lead this U.S. Mission to the UN in New York from 2009 to 2013.

January 24

1991 On this day in 1991, Ambassador Leonard Spearman presented his credentials to the leadership in Lesotho, officially beginning his tenure in-residence, as U.S. Ambassador to this southern African nation. Spearman was a university educator, leader, public servant, and a diplomat who served as U.S. Ambassador to Rwanda from 1988 to 1990, and then to Lesotho from 1990 to 1993.

1997 On this day in 1997, Ambassador Terence Todman departed his post in Costa Rica. Born in the U.S. Virgin Islands, Todman was a military veteran and career diplomat who has the distinction of being a U.S. Ambassador on six separate occasions, more than any other Black American in history. His ambassadorial service included: Chad from 1969 to 1972, Guinea from 1972 to 1975, Costa Rica from 1974 to 1977, Spain from 1978 to 1983, Denmark from 1983 to 1989, and Argentina from 1989 to 1993.

January 25

1993 On this day in 1993, the book *Dream Maker, Dream Breaker: The World of Thurgood Marshall*, written by Ambassador Carl T. Rowan, was first published. Rowan was a military veteran, journalist, and diplomat who served as U.S. Ambassador to Finland from 1963 to 1964. Ambassador Rowan also wrote a biography about Jackie Robinson.

January 26

2009 On this day in 2009, Ambassador Susan Rice presented her credentials at the U.S. Mission to the United Nations in New York, officially beginning her tenure in-residence as the leader of the U.S. Mission to the UN in New York. Rice was a Rhodes Scholar, foreign policy expert, and diplomat who served as U.S. Permanent Representative to the United Nations with the rank of Ambassador from 2009 to 2013.

2008 On this day in 2008, Ambassador John Withers was the subject of an article by the "Tirana Times" news outlet in Albania. The article covered a recent speech by Ambassador Withers speech, where he assured Albania that the U.S. policy toward the nation had not changed, and the U.S., as it transitioned from one presidential administration to another, would remain a strong friend to Albania and continue to support its efforts to join NATO. Ambassador Withers was a career diplomat who served as U.S. Ambassador to Albania from 2007 to 2010.

Major Milestone Moment

January 27

On this day in 2000, an official U.S. stamp was issued bearing the name and image of **Ambassador Patricia Roberts Harris**. Harris was an attorney, public servant, and diplomat who would become the first Black American woman to ever serve as a U.S. Ambassador, doing so in Luxembourg, from 1965 to 1967. She was later appointed as the Dean of the Howard University School of Law (1969), the school's first female Dean. She also served as U.S. Secretary of Housing and Urban Development (1977), making her the first Black American woman to ever hold a Cabinet-level post, and the first to ever be part of the Presidential Line of Succession.

January 27

1977 On this day in 1977, President Jimmy Carter nominated Andrew Young to be Permanent Representative of the U.S. to the United Nations (UN) with the rank of Ambassador. Following Senate confirmation, he would become the (1977-79), the first Black American to ever hold this role and rank at the UN on behalf of the U.S.A. He would lead the U.S. Mission to the UN in New York from 1977 to 1979.

1993 On this day in 1993, Ambassador Edward Perkins departed from his post as leader of the U.S. Mission to the United Nations in New York. Perkins was a military veteran and career diplomat who served as U.S. Ambassador on four separate occasions, including Liberia from 1985 to 1986, South Africa from 1986 to 1989, the United Nations (UN) from 1992 to 1993, and Australia from 1993 to 1996.

1999 On this day in 1999, Ambassador George Staples presented his credentials to the leadership of Rwanda, officially beginning his tenure in-residence as leader of the U.S. Mission to that African nation. Staples was a military veteran and career diplomat who served as U.S. Ambassador to Rwanda from 1998 to 2001, and to Cameroon and Equatorial Guinea from 2001 to 2004.

2015 On this day in 2015, Ambassador Pamela Spratlen presented her credentials to the leadership in Uzbekistan, officially beginning her tenure in-residence as leader of the U.S. Mission to that country. Spratlen was a career diplomat who served as U.S. Ambassador to the Kyrgyz Republic from 2011 to 2014, and to Uzbekistan from 2015 to 2018.

January 28

1957 On this day in 1957, Suzan Johnson Cook was born in New York, New York. Johnson Cook was a religious leader, motivational speaker, and diplomat who would serve as U.S. Ambassador-at-Large for International Religious

Freedom from 2011 to 2013. She would be the first woman and the first Black American to hold this position.

1981 On this day in 1981, Ambassador Ulric St. Claire Haynes departed from his post as leader of the U.S. Mission in Algeria, where he had served as U.S. Ambassador since 1977. During his time as Ambassador in Algeria, he was instrumental in the negotiations for the release of the U.S. hostages in Iran.

2002 On this day in 2002, Ambassador Wanda Nesbitt presented her credentials in Madagascar, officially beginning her tenure in-residence, as the leader of the U.S. Mission to this African island nation. Nesbitt was a career diplomat who served the U.S. as Ambassador to three nations: Madagascar from 2001 to 2004, Côte d'Ivoire from 2007 to 2010, and Namibia from 2010 to 2013.

2003 On this day in 2003, Ambassador Joseph Huggins presented his credentials to the leadership in Botswana, officially beginning his tenure in-residence as leader of the U.S. Mission to this southern African nation. Huggins was a career diplomat who served as U.S. Ambassador to Botswana from 2002 to 2005.

Major Milestone Moment

January 29

On this day in 2020, the International Student House of Washington, DC (ISH-DC) welcomed an esteemed group of retired U.S. Ambassadors for a panel discussion at their historic R Street, NW location in the nation's capital. The event, in partnership with the Una Chapman Cox Foundation and the Association of Black American Ambassadors (ABAA), was moderated by the Foundation's Executive Director, Ambassador Lino Gutierrez, and featured **Ambassadors Edward J. Perkins, Johnny Young, Pamela Spratlen, and Frankie Reed**, who shared insights and observations reflecting their decades of experience in the U.S. Foreign Service and as American diplomatic leaders. Together, their experience included a combined total of 15 ambassadorial postings and senior appointments in the U.S. State Department.

January 30

1926 On this day in 1926, Horace G. Dawson was born in Augusta, Georgia. Dawson was a military veteran, career diplomat, and university educator who would serve as U.S. Ambassador to Botswana from 1979 to 1982. Among his many career accomplishments, Ambassador Dawson founded the Howard University Bunche International Affairs Center in 1992.

1977 On this day in 1977, Ambassador Andrew Young presented his credentials to the leadership of the United Nations (UN), officially beginning his tenure in-residence, as the leader of the U.S. Mission to the UN in New York. Young was a minister, civil rights activist, public servant, and diplomat who served as U.S. Permanent Representative to the United Nations (UN) with the rank of Ambassador from 1977 to 1979. He was the first Black American to ever hold this role and rank. He was also a close advisor to Dr. Martin Luther King, Jr.

2002 On this day in 2002, President George W. Bush nominated James D. McGee to be U.S. Ambassador to Swaziland. Following Senate confirmation, Ambassador McGee would lead the U.S. Mission to his Sub-Saharan African nation until 2004.

January 31

2015 On this day in 2015, Ambassador Adrienne O'Neal departed from her post as leader of the U.S. Mission in Cape Verde. O'Neal was a career diplomat who served as U.S. Ambassador to Cape Verde from 2011 to 2015.

CHAPTER 3:
FEBRUARY

February 1
1921 On this day in 1921, William Beverly Carter was born in Coatesville, Pennsylvania. Carter was a journalist and career diplomat who served as U.S. Ambassador to Tanzania from 1972 to 1975, to Liberia from 1976 to 1979, and At-Large as Liaison Responsible for State and Local Government relations from 1979 to 1981.

February 2
2021 On this day in 2021, the *Associated Press* reported that President Joe Biden intended to nominate Ambassador Brian Nichols as his top envoy for Latin America (Assistant Secretary for Western Hemisphere Affairs). The article described Nichols as "a veteran Black American diplomat who, while on a sensitive assignment in Zimbabwe, spoke out against police brutality in the U.S. following the death of George Floyd." Ambassador Nichols was a career diplomat who served as U.S. Ambassador to Peru from 2014 to 2017 and to Zimbabwe from 2018 to 2021.

February 3
2000 On this day in 2000, Ambassador Gregory Johnson presented his credentials to the leadership of the Kingdom of Swaziland, officially beginning his tenure in-residence as the leader of the U.S. Mission in that southern African nation. Johnson was a career diplomat who, after being appointed in 1999 and confirmed by the U.S. Senate that year, would serve as U.S. Ambassador in Swaziland (now called Eswatini) until 2001.

February 4
2015 On this day in 2015, Ambassador Marcia Bernicat presented her credentials to the leadership in Bangladesh, officially beginning her tenure in-residence, as the leader of the U.S. Mission in that country. Bernicat was a career

diplomat who served as U.S. Ambassador to Senegal and concurrently Guinea-Bissau from 2008 to 2011, and then to Bangladesh from 2015 to 2018.

Major Milestone Moment

February 5

On this day in 1921, the First Standard Bank opened in Louisville, Kentucky, becoming the state's first Black-owned bank. Among its establishers was **Richard Jones**, who would later serve as U.S. Ambassador to Liberia from 1955 to 1959. Jones was only the third Black American in our nation's history to serve as a U.S. Ambassador. Ambassador Jones was also a decorated military leader, having served in both World War I and II. He would earn the rank of Brigadier General and ultimately became the 1st Illinois National Guardsman to have a National Guard Armory named after him – the General Richard L. Jones Armory, which was dedicated in October 1970 in Chicago, Illinois.

February 5

1998 On this day in 1988, President Ronald Regan nominated Leonard Spearman, Sr., to be U.S. Ambassador to Rwanda. Following Senate confirmation, Ambassador Spearman would lead the U.S. Mission in this Sub-Saharan African nation from 1988 to 1990.

February 6

1940 On this day in 1940, Johnny Young was born in Savannah, Georgia. Young was a career diplomat who would serve as U.S. Ambassador on four separate occasions, including: to Sierra Leone from 1989 to 1992; Togo from 1994 to 1997; Bahrain from 1997 to 2001; and Slovenia from 2001 to 2004. With these four separate ambassadorial appointments, Ambassador Young was in rare company, as there was only one other Black American who had more appointments, and only one other had the same number (4) of appointments as did Young.

February 7

2009 On this day in 2009, Ambassador C. Steven McGann presented his credentials to the leadership in Fiji, officially beginning his tenure in-residence as leader of the U.S. Mission in this Pacific Island nation. Ambassador McGann would also simultaneously serve in the same capacity to four other East Asian and Pacific Island nations including Kiribati, Nauru, Tonga, and Tuvalu, until 2011.

February 8

1964 On this day in 1964, Ambassador Carl Rowan ended his tenure as U.S Ambassador to Finland. Rowan was a military veteran, journalist, author, and diplomat, who shortly after ending his time as U.S. Ambassador in Finland, became Director of the U.S. Information Agency (USIA). This made him the first Black American to lead that agency, which at the time was responsible for U.S. public diplomacy abroad. In this role, he would also be the first Black American to hold a seat on the National Security Council, on which the USIA Director sat.

February 9

1979 On this day in 1979, William Beverly Carter was appointed U.S. Ambassador-at-Large with the responsibility as Liaison for State and Local Government. After Senate confirmation, Ambassador Carter would serve in this role until 1981. Carter was a journalist and career diplomat who, in addition to his role as Ambassador-at-Large, had previously served as U.S. Ambassador to Tanzania from 1972 to 1975, and Liberia from 1976 to 1979.

1994 On this day in 1994, Sidney Williams was appointed as U.S. Ambassador to the Bahamas. Following Senate confirmation, Ambassador Williams served in this role until 1998. Williams was an athlete, public servant, businessman, and diplomat who was the first Black American to ever serve as U.S. Ambassador to this Caribbean nation.

February 10

1910 On this day in 1910, John Morrow was born in Hackensack, New Jersey. Morrow was a scholar, university educator, and diplomat, who became America's first leader at two key international postings – the African nation of Guinea and the United Nations Educational, Scientific, and Cultural Organization (UNESCO). Firstly, he became the first ever U.S. Ambassador to the African nation of Guinea, serving there from 1959 to 1961. Later, with the rank of Minister, he became the first ever U.S. Permanent Representative to United Nations Educational, Scientific, and Cultural Organization (UNESCO) from 1961 to 1963.

February 11

2015 On this day in 2015, Ambassador Sue Brown ended her term as U.S. Ambassador to Montenegro. Brown was a career diplomat who had served as U.S. Ambassador to this Balkan region nation in Europe from 2011 to 2015.

February 12

1975 On this day in 1975, Ambassador Theodore Britton, Jr. presented his credentials to the leadership in Barbados and Grenada, officially beginning his tenure in-residence as the leader of the U.S. Mission in this Caribbean nation. Britton was a military veteran, public servant, and diplomat who served as U.S. Ambassador to Barbados and Grenada until 1977.

1990 On this day in 1990, Ambassador Cynthia Shephard Perry presented her credentials to the leadership in Burundi, officially beginning her tenure in-residence as the leader of the U.S. Mission in this Asian nation. Perry was a university educator and diplomat who served as U.S. Ambassador to Sierra Leone from 1986 to 1989, following her role as Ambassador to Burundi, for which she served until 1993.

February 13

2003 On this day in 2003, Ambassador Robin Sanders presented her credentials to the leadership of the Republic of the Congo, officially beginning her tenure in-residence as the leader of the U.S. Mission in this African nation. Sanders was a career diplomat who served as U.S. Ambassador to the Congo from 2002 to 2005, and later to Nigeria from 2007 to 2010. Her appointment as U.S. Ambassador to Nigeria made her the first Black American woman to serve as Ambassador to Africa's most populous nation.

February 14

2019 On this day in 2019, Ambassador Linda Thomas-Greenfield co-authored an article in *African Focus*, entitled "From Wakanda to Reality: Building Mutual Prosperity Between African Americans and Africa." Ambassador Thomas-Greenfield was a university educator and career diplomat who served as U.S. Ambassador to Liberia from 2008 to 2012 and the United Nations beginning in 2021, where she still was serving at the time of writing this book.

February 15

1979 On this day in 1979, Ambassador William Beverly Carter officially began his tenure as Ambassador-at-Large with the responsibility as Liaison for State and Local Government. Carter was a journalist and career diplomat who served as U.S. Ambassador to Tanzania from 1972 to 1975, to Liberia from 1976 to 1979, and in this role as Liaison with State and Local Government with rank of Ambassador-At-Large from 1979 to 1981.

February 16

1990 On this day in 1990, Jerome Holland was appointed as U.S. Ambassador to Sweden. Holland was an athlete, sociologist, university leader, businessman, and diplomat who would serve in this capacity as U.S. Ambassador to Sweden from 1970 to 1972. Prior to that, from 1935 to 1939, he had been the first Black American to play football at the Ivy League's Cornell University where he was a two-time All American. Later in his career, after his ambassadorship, he would also become the first Black American to be elected to sit on the Board of the New York Stock Exchange, doing so from 1972 to 1980.

February 17

2012 On this day in 2012, President Barack Obama nominated Makila James to be U.S. Ambassador to Swaziland (now called Eswatini). Following Senate confirmation, Ambassador James would officially become U.S. Ambassador to that Sub-Saharan African nation, serving in that role until 2015.

February 18

1982 On this day in 1982, Ambassador Gerald Thomas presented his credentials to the leadership of Guyana, officially beginning his tenure in-residence as the leader of the U.S. Mission in this South American country. Thomas was a military veteran, career military officer (held the rank of Rear Admiral), university educators, and diplomat who served as U.S. Ambassador to the Guyana from 1981 to 1983 and to Kenya from 1983 to 1989.

February 19
2005 On this day in 2005, Ambassador Francis Taylor ended his term as Assistant Secretary of State in the Bureau of Diplomatic Security & Director of the Office of Foreign Missions at the U.S. Department of State. Taylor, a military leader, intelligence and security expert, and diplomat, had also previously served as Coordinator of Counterterrorism and Director, Office to Monitor and Combat Trafficking in Persons with the rank of Ambassador from 2001 to 2004.

February 20
1964 On this day in 1964, Ambassador Will Mercer Cook gave a speech to the American Society of African Culture, praising African novelists for their contribution to the world of literature. Cook was a scholar, university educator, and diplomat who became the first Black American to have more than one ambassadorial appointment in his career. This occurred when, following his service as U.S. Ambassador to Niger ended in 1964, Cook was then appointed as U.S. Ambassador to Senegal and also to The Gambia. He would serve as U.S. Ambassador to both African nations until 1966.

2024 On this day in 2024, Ambassador Vernelle Trim FitzPatrick met with Gabon coup leader General Brice Clotaire Oligui Nguema six months after his September 2023 swearing in as interim president of the country. Ambassador FitzPatrick, the U.S. Ambassador to Gabon, met with Nguema to reiterate U.S. interest in continuing strong economic and diplomatic relations with the central African nation, despite recent sanctions that had been imposed on the coup leader. She urged Nguema toward a quick return to constitutional order. Ambassador FitzPatrick was a career diplomat who began serving as U.S. Ambassador to Gabon in 2023 and was still in this leadership role at the time of writing in 2025.

February 21

2001 On this day in 2021, Ambassador Dereck Hogan, Ambassador Reuben Brigety, and Ambassador Pamela Spratlen shared the virtual state with one another in a conversation moderated by the author (Dr. Carlton McLellan) and co-hosted by the Black Professional in International Affairs, Association of Black American Ambassadors (ABAA), Congressional Black Caucus Institute, and Thursday Luncheon Group. The conversation titled "Sitting at the Head of the U.S. Diplomatic Table: Black American Ambassadors Speak was part of the Black History Month celebrations and had over 100 participants. Ambassador Dereck Hogan was a career diplomat who served as U.S. Ambassador to Moldova (2018-2021). Ambassador Reuben Brigety was a military veteran, university educator, international humanitarian expert, and diplomat who served as U.S. Representative to the African Union (AU), with the rank of Ambassador from 2013 to 2015, and later as U.S. Ambassador to South Africa from 2021 to 2025. Finally, Ambassador Pamela Spratlen was a career diplomat who served as U.S. Ambassador to the Kyrgyz Republic from 2011 to 2014, and to Uzbekistan from 2015 to 2018.

2002 On this day in 2002, Ambassador James McGee presented his credentials to the leadership in Swaziland (now called Eswatini), officially beginning his tenure in-residence, as the leader of the U.S. Mission in this southern African country. McGee was a military veteran and career diplomat who served as U.S. Ambassador to Swaziland from 2002 to 2004, Madagascar and concurrently The Comoros from 2004 to 2007, and to Zimbabwe from 2007 to 2009.

February 22

2021 On this day in 2021, the career of Ambassador Irving Hicks, Sr., is celebrated in an op-ed written by his son Irving Hicks, Jr. Published in the U.S. Department of State's Dip-Note, the article is entitled "60 Years of Service: An

American Diplomat's Short Story." It gracefully tells the story of how the careers of both Hicks (Sr. and Jr.) in service to U.S. foreign affairs and national security, were deeply influenced by "inflection points in American history." Ambassador Hicks, Sr., was a career diplomat who served as U.S. Ambassador to the Seychelles from 1985 to 1987, the United Nation's Security Council with the rank of Ambassador from 1992 to 1993, and Ethiopia from 1994 to 1996.

February 23
1975 On this day in 1975, Ambassador John Reinhardt departed from his post as leader of the U.S. Mission in Nigeria. Reinhardt was a military veteran, career diplomat, and university educator who served as U.S. Ambassador to Nigeria from 1971 to 1975, becoming the first Black American to lead, as Ambassador, the U.S. Mission in Africa's most populous nation.

February 24
1980 On this day in 1980, Ambassador Mabel Murphy Smythe departed her post as leader of the U.S. Mission in Cameroon. During a portion of this time, she also concurrently served as U.S. Ambassador to Equatorial Guinea. Ambassador Smythe was an educator, public servant, and diplomat, and she was also one half of the first Black husband and wife union to hold ambassadorial postings as her husband, Hugh Smythe, had been U.S. Ambassador to Syria from 1965 to 1967.

Major Milestone Moment

February 25

On this day in 2021, **Ambassador Linda Thomas-Greenfield** presented her credentials to the leadership at the headquarters of the United Nations (UN) in New York, officially beginning her tenure as the chief U.S. diplomat to this global body. Ambassador Thomas-Greenfield was a university educator and career diplomat who had previously served as U.S. Ambassador to Liberia from 2008 to 2012. Her tenure at the UN would run from 2021 to 2025. With this appointment, she joined a distinguished group of Black Americans who had previously held this role, including: **Andrew Young** from 1977 to 1979; **Donald McHenry** from 1979 to 1981; **Edward Perkins** from 1992 to 1993; and, **Susan Rice** from 2009 to 2013.

February 26

2018 On this day in 2018, Ambassador Cynthia Akuetteh officially completed her service as U.S. Ambassador to the Sub-Saharan African nations of Gabon and São Tomé and Príncipe. Akuetteh was a career diplomat who had served as the leader of the U.S. diplomatic missions to both these nations since 2014.

Major Milestone Moment

February 27

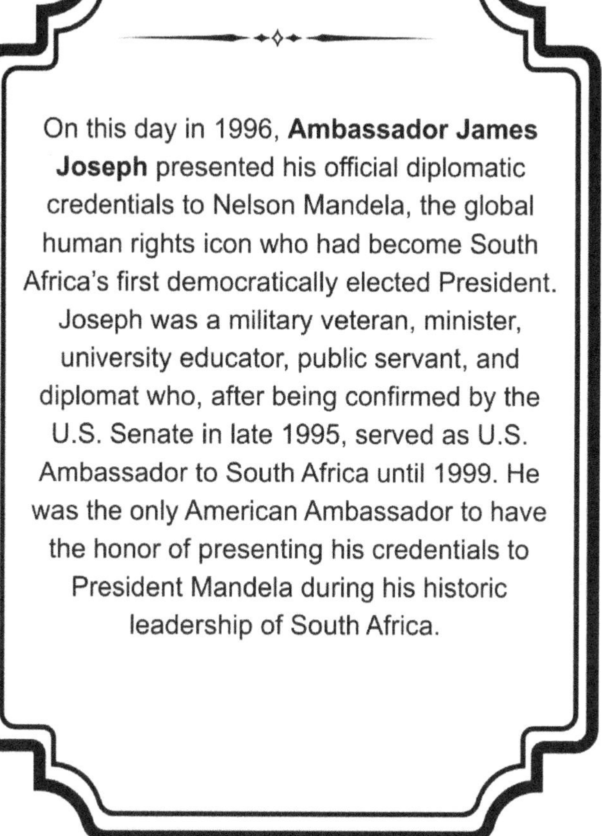

On this day in 1996, **Ambassador James Joseph** presented his official diplomatic credentials to Nelson Mandela, the global human rights icon who had become South Africa's first democratically elected President. Joseph was a military veteran, minister, university educator, public servant, and diplomat who, after being confirmed by the U.S. Senate in late 1995, served as U.S. Ambassador to South Africa until 1999. He was the only American Ambassador to have the honor of presenting his credentials to President Mandela during his historic leadership of South Africa.

February 27

1981 On this day in 1981, Ambassador Anne Forrester Holloway departed her post as leader of the U.S. Mission in Mali. Holloway was a scholar, activist, university educator, and diplomat who served as U.S. Ambassador to Mali from 1979 to 1981.

February 28

1974 On this day in 1974, David Bolen was appointed as U.S. Ambassador, concurrently, to Botswana, Lesotho, and Swaziland. As a student athlete in college, Bolen had also been the first ever University of Colorado at Boulder athlete to make a U.S. Olympic Team. He was a member of the 1948 U.S.A. team, and he finished fourth in the 400-meter run at the London games. Bolen then embarked on a diplomatic career which included his 1974 appointment as U.S. Ambassador to the nations of Botswana, Lesotho, and Swaziland, where he served until 1976; and a 1977 appointment as Ambassador to the German Democratic Republic (East Germany), serving there until 1980.

1993 On this day in 1993, Ambassador Cynthia Shephard Perry departed from her post as leader of the U.S. Mission in Burundi. Perry was a university educator and diplomat who served as U.S. Ambassador to Sierra Leone from 1986 to 1989 and then to Burundi from 1989 to 1993.

Major Milestone Moment

February 29

On this day in 2000, a U.S. House of Representatives Special Order was written and entered into the records as H522 and titled "Heritage and Horizons: The African American Legacy and the Challenges of the 21st Century". It which outlined in detail the life and legacy of **Ambassador Carl Stokes**. Ambassador Stokes was a military veteran, attorney, public servant, and diplomat who served as U.S. Ambassador to the Seychelles from 1994 to 1995. Prior to this, Ambassador Stokes had also been elected Mayor of Cleveland, Ohio (1967), making him the first Black mayor of a major U.S. city.

CHAPTER 4:
MARCH

March 1

1946 On this day in 1946, Robert C. Perry was born in Durham, North Carolina. Perry was a career diplomat who would serve as U.S. Ambassador to the Central African Republic from 1998 to 2001.

Major Milestone Moment

March 2

On this day in 1961, President John F. Kennedy nominated **Clifton R. Wharton, Sr.**, as U.S. Ambassador to Norway. After Senate Confirmation, Wharton would become the first Black American to serve as U.S. Ambassador to a European nation (1961-1964). Prior to his ambassadorial appointment, Wharton had been the first Black American to ever pass the U.S. Foreign Service Exam, which was the exam required for entrance into the professional diplomatic service of the U.S. Department of State (1961).

March 3

1942 On this day in 1942, Sidney Williams was born in Shreveport, Louisiana. Williams was an athlete, public servant, businessman, and diplomat who would serve as U.S. Ambassador to the Bahamas from 1994 to 1998, the first Black American to hold that post. Brown had a professional football career, having been drafted by the Cleveland Browns. In his rookie season as a defensive lineman he played alongside the legendary Jim Brown, helping the team to the 1964 National Football League (NFL) Championship.

March 4

2011 On this day in 2011, Sue K. Brown was nominated by President Barack Obama as the U.S. Ambassador to Montenegro. After Senate confirmation, Ambassador Brown would serve in this leadership role from 2011 to 2015.

March 5

1920 On this day in 1920, Charles Nelson was born in Battle Creek, Michigan. Nelson was a military veteran, public servant, diplomat, and university educator who would serve as U.S. Ambassador to Botswana, Lesotho, and Swaziland from 1971 to 1974, simultaneously making him the first ever American Chief of Mission with the full rank of Ambassador, to these three African nations.

March 6

1947 On this day in 1947, Howard Jeter was born in Union, South Carolina. Jeter was a career diplomat who served as U.S. Ambassador to Botswana from 1993 to 1996, and to Nigeria from 2000 to 2003.

1968 On this day in 1968, Nicole Avant was born in Beverly Hills, California. Avant was an entertainment industry executive, fundraiser, and diplomat who would serve as U.S. Ambassador to the Bahamas from 2009 to 2011.

March 7
1974 On this day in 1974, Jet magazine published an article about the visit by the Jackson 5 singing group to Senegal. In that article, Ambassador O. Rudolph Aggrey, who was currently serving as U.S. Ambassador to Senegal, attended the event and remarked that the visit was "...a milestone in cultural relations between America and Africa. A link which was lost and now is found..." During the visit, the young superstar Michael Jackson also presented Ambassador Aggrey with one of the group's gold records.

March 8
1920 On this day in 1920, John Reinhardt was born in Knoxville, Tennessee. Reinhardt was a military veteran, career diplomat, and university educator who served as U.S. Ambassador to Nigeria from 1971 to 1975, becoming the first Black American to lead the U.S. Mission in Africa's most populous nation.

March 9
1963 On this day in 1963, Carl Rowan was nominated by President John F. Kennedy to be U.S. Ambassador to Finland. After Senate confirmation, Ambassador Rowan would serve in this leadership post from 1963-1964.

1982 On this day in 1982, President Ronald Reagan appointed Howard K. Walker as U.S. Ambassador to Togo. After Senate confirmation, Walker led the U.S. Mission in Togo as Ambassador from 1982 to 1984.

March 10
2015 On this day in 2015, Stafford Fitzgerald Haney testified before the U.S. Senate Foreign Relations Committee as the nominee to be U.S. Ambassador to Costa Rica. After the hearing, Haney was confirmed and would go on to serve as U.S. Ambassador to this Central American nation from 2015 to 2017.

Major Milestone Moment

March 11

On this day in 1911, **Edward Dudley** was born in South Boston, Virginia. Dudley was an attorney, civil rights advocate, judge, and diplomat who would become the first Black American to ever hold the title and rank of U.S. Ambassador, serving in Liberia from 1949 to 1953. In addition to this distinction as America's first Black Ambassador, Dudley also worked alongside future Supreme Court Justice–and America's first Black Supreme Court Justice – Thurgood Marshall in the legal department of the National Association for the Advancement of Colored People (NAACP). Together they led many landmark civil rights cases fighting against jim crow segregationist laws, on behalf of the NAACP.

Major Milestone Moment

March 12

On this day, three different Black Americans who would go on to become U.S. Ambassadors were born. On this day in 1932, **Andrew Young** was born in New Orleans, Louisiana. Young was a minister, civil rights activist, public servant, and diplomat who served as the U.S. Permanent Representative to the United Nations (UN) with the rank of Ambassador, from 1977 to 1979. He was the first Black American to ever hold this role and rank. On this day in 1935, **James Joseph** was born in Plaisance, Louisiana. Joseph was a military veteran, minister, university educator, public servant, and diplomat who would serve as U.S. Ambassador to South Africa from 1995 to 1999. He was the first and only American Ambassador to ever present his credentials to Nelson Mandela, South Africa's global human rights icon and first democratically elected Present. Finally, on this day in 1948, **James Gadsden** was born in Charleston, South Carolina. Gadsden was a career diplomat who would serve as U.S. Ambassador to Iceland from 2002 to 2005.

March 12

1935 On this day in 1935, James Joseph was born in Plaisance, Louisiana. Joseph was a military veteran, minister, university educator, public servant, and diplomat who would serve as U.S. Ambassador to South Africa from 1995 to 1999. Upon arrival in South Africa as U.S. Ambassador, he presented his diplomatic credentials to President Nelson Mandela (February 27, 1996), making him the first and only American Ambassador to ever present his credentials to South Africa's global human rights icon and first democratically elected President (Mandela).

1948 On this day in 1948, James Gadsden was born in Charleston, South Carolina. Gadsden was a career diplomat who would serve as U.S. Ambassador to Iceland from 2002 to 2005.

Major Milestone Moment

March 13

On this day in 1926, **Terence Todman** was born in St. Thomas, U.S. Virgin Islands. Todman was a military veteran and career diplomat who had the distinction of being a U.S. Ambassador more than any other Black American in history (six total), including: to Chad from 1969 to 1972; Guinea from 1972 to 1975; Costa Rica from 1974 to 1977; Spain from 1978 to 1983; Denmark from 1983 to 1989; and, Argentina from 1989 to 1993. Todman's diplomatic leadership and his profound contributions to American diplomatic relations was recognized by the U.S. government when in 1989, he earned promotion to the rank of Career Ambassador, making him the first Black American to earn this rank – the diplomatic equivalent to a Four Star General.

March 14

2022 On this day in 2022, U.S. Ambassador to the United Nations Linda Thomas-Greenfield met with Polish Minister of Foreign Affairs Zbigniew Rau to discuss the rapid increase in refugee flows from Ukraine into Poland and other neighboring countries because of Russia's war against Ukraine. Thomas-Greenfield was a university educator and career diplomat who served as U.S. Ambassador to Liberia (2008-2012) and to the United Nations, where she began and 2021 and was still serving at the time of this writing.

March 15

2013 On this day in 2013, Ambassador Ronald Kirk, the first Black American to serve as U.S. Trade Representative, where he held the rank of Ambassador, finished his tenure after having served since 2009 as the lead U.S. trade negotiator for President Barack Obama. Kirk was an attorney, public servant, and diplomat in addition to serving as U.S. Trade Representative with the rank of Ambassador from 2009 to 2013. He had also previously served as the Mayor of the City of Dallas, Texas from 1995 to 2002.

March 16

1938 On this day in 1938, Irvin Hicks, Sr., was born in Baltimore, Maryland. Hicks was a career diplomat who served as U.S. Ambassador to the Seychelles from 1985 to 1987, to the United Nations' Security Council with the rank of Ambassador from 1992 to 1993, and to Ethiopia from 1994 to 1996.

March 17

1949 On this day in 1949, the U.S. Senate confirmed Edward Dudley as U.S. Ambassador to Liberia, officially making him the first Black American to receive such confirmation with the title and rank of Ambassador in U.S. history.

March 18

2009 On this day in 2009, Ambassador Ronald Kirk was confirmed as U.S. Trade Representative with the rank of Ambassador by the U.S. Senate. Ambassador Kirk would be the first Black American to ever serve as U.S. Trade Representative.

March 19

2010 On this day in 2010, Ambassador Harry Thomas, Jr. was nominated by President Barack Obama to be U.S. Ambassador to the Philippines. After Senate confirmation, he served as the leader of the U.S. Mission in Southeast Asian nation until 2013.

March 20

2019 On this day in 2019, Ambassador Gerald Thomas passed away. Ambassador Thomas was a military veteran, career military officer, university educator, and diplomat who served as U.S. Ambassador to the South American nation of Guyana from 1981 to 1983 and to Kenya from 1983 to 1989. He had also been only the 2nd African American in history to obtain the rank of Rear Admiral in the U.S. Navy.

March 21

2019 On this day in 2019, Ambassador Harriet Elam-Thomas delivered remarks on the topic of "Civility in Public Affairs" and about her memoir entitled *Diversifying Diplomacy* at a public policy forum hosted by the Paul Simon Public Policy Institute, Southern Illinois University Carbondale, Illinois. Elam-Thomas was a university educator and career diplomat who served as U.S. Ambassador to Senegal and Guinea-Bissau concurrently from 1999 to 2002.

March 22

1932 On this day in 1932, Ronald Palmer was born in Uniontown, Pennsylvania. Ambassador Palmer was a career diplomat and university educator who would serve as a U.S. Ambassador on three occasions, including: to Togo from 1976 to 1978; Malaysia from 1981 to 1983; and, Mauritius from 1986 to 1989.

March 23

1985 On this day in 1985, Ambassador Patricia Roberts Harris passed away from breast cancer. Ambassador Harris was an attorney, public servant, and diplomat who became the first Black American woman to ever serve as a U.S. Ambassador, serving as such in Luxembourg from 1965 to 1967.

March 24

1993 On this day in 1993, Ambassador Joseph Segars presented his credentials to the leadership of Cape Verde, officially beginning his tenure in-residence, as leader of the U.S. Mission in this African nation. Segars was an educator and diplomat who served as U.S. Ambassador to Cape Verde from 1992 to 1996.

March 25

2018 On this day in 2018, Ambassador Harry Thomas, Jr., departed from his post as leader of the U.S. Mission to Zimbabwe. Thomas was a career diplomat who served as U.S. Ambassador to Bangladesh from 2003 to 2005, the Philippines from 2010 to 2013, and Zimbabwe (2016-2018).

March 26

2021 On this day in 2021, the White House officially released a statement that President Joe Biden intended to nominate Ambassador Brian A. Nichols to serve as Assistant Secretary of State for Western Hemisphere Affairs. Ambassador Nichols was a career diplomat who served as U.S. Ambassador to Peru from 2014 to 2017 and to Zimbabwe from 2018 to 2021.

March 27

1994 On this day in 1994, Ambassador Sidney Williams presented his credentials to the leadership of the Bahamas, officially beginning his tenure in-residence as the leader of the U.S. Mission in this Caribbean Island nation. Williams was an athlete, public servant, businessman, and diplomat, and in this role as U.S. Ambassador to the Bahamas, he would be the first Black American to hold that post, serving from 1994 to 1998.

Major Milestone Moment

March 28

On this day in 2018, the media powerhouse Netflix announced the appointment of **Ambassador Susan Rice** to its Board of Directors. Ambassador Rice was a Rhodes Scholar, foreign policy expert, and diplomat who served as U.S. Permanent Representative to the United Nations with the rank of Ambassador from 2009 to 2013. She would also serve as National Security Advisor in the Obama Administration from 2013 to 2017, and later as Director of the U.S. Domestic Policy Council in President Joe Biden's administration from 2021 to 2023.

March 29

2012 On this day in 2012, Gina Abercrombie-Winstanley was confirmed by the U.S. Senate as the U.S. Ambassador to Malta. Ambassador Abercrombie-Winstanley would serve as the leader of the U.S. Mission in this Mediterranean, European island nation from 2012 to 2016. She had previously been the first American woman to lead a U.S. consulate, as Counsel General, in the gender conservative Kingdom of Saudi Arabia from 2002 to 2004.

March 30

1903 On this day in 1903, Will Mercer Cook was born in Washington, DC. Cook was a scholar, university educator, and diplomat who would become the first Black American to have multiple ambassadorial appointments. He served as U.S. Ambassador to Niger from 1961 to 1964; and to Senegal from 1964 to 1966, during which time he was also accredited to The Gambia.

March 31

1997 On this day in 1997, Ambassador Mosina Jordan officially ended her term as U.S. Ambassador to the Central African Republic (CAR). Jordan was an international development expert and career diplomat who had led the U.S. Mission in this sub-Saharan African nation since 1995. While in CAR, there was a military mutiny, and the unrest and violence caused Ambassador Jordan and her Embassy staff to be evacuated. She was evacuated to nearby Cameroon, where she continued to lead the U.S. Mission in CAR from afar.

CHAPTER 5:
APRIL

April 1

1958 On this day in 1958, Ambassador Joel Danies was born in Jacmel, Haiti. Danies was a career diplomat who would serve as U.S. Ambassador to Gabon and concurrently to São Tomé and Principe from 2017 to 2019.

April 2

2012 On this day in 2012, Ambassador Larry Palmer was appointed as U.S. Ambassador to Barbados, East Caribbean, and the Organization of Eastern Caribbean States. After Senate confirmation, he would serve in this role until 2016. Palmer was a career diplomat and a university educator who had also previously served as U.S. Ambassador to Honduras from 2002 to 2005.

April 3

1918 On this day in 1918, Ambassador Mabel Murphy Smythe was born in Montgomery, Alabama. Murphy Smyth was a university educator, public servant, and diplomat who served as U.S. Ambassador to Cameroon from 1977 to 1980, and concurrently to Equatorial Guinea from 1979 to 1980.

April 4

2012 On this day in 2012, Ambassador Ertharin Cousin officially ended her term as U.S. Representative to the United Nations (UN) Agencies for Food and Agriculture in Rome. Cousin was an attorney, a global hunger and food expert, and a diplomat who served in this role, with the rank of Ambassador, from 2009 to 2012.

April 5

1938 On this day in 1938, Ambassador Shirley Barnes was born in St. Augustine, Florida. Barnes was a career diplomat who served as U.S. Ambassador to Madagascar from 1998 to 2001.

April 6

2016 On this day in 2016, Ambassador O. Rudolph Aggrey passed away. Ambassador Aggrey was a journalist, career diplomat, and university educator who served as U.S. Ambassador to Senegal and The Gambia from 1973 to 1977 and Romania from 1977 to 1981.

April 7

1944 On this day in 1944, Ambassador Johnnie Carson was born in Chicago, Illinois. Carson was a career diplomat who served the United States as Ambassador on three separate occasions, including to Uganda from 1991 to 1994; Zimbabwe from 1995 to 1997; and Kenya from 1999 to 2003.

April 8

2019 On this day in 2019, well-known civil rights leader and former advisor to Martin Luther King Jr., Ambassador Andrew Young, spoke at The Summit on Race in America at the LBJ Presidential Library in Austin, Texas. Young was a minister, civil rights activist, public servant, and diplomat who served as U.S. Permanent Representative to the United Nations (UN) with the rank of Ambassador from 1977 to 1979, the first Black American to ever hold this role and rank. He had also served as Mayor of the City of Atlanta from 1981 to 1990.

April 9

2022 On this day in 2022, Wired JA News published an article announcing that President Joe Biden had nominated Nick Perry, as U.S. Ambassador to Jamaica. Upon Senate confirmation on March 10, 2022, Perry, a career public servant who had served the city and state of New York in multiple roles, would be the first Jamaican born U.S. citizen to hold this role as the leader of the U.S. diplomatic mission in this Caribbean Island nation. He would serve in this role until 2025.

April 10

1955 On this day in 1955, Ambassador Jessie Locker passed away in Monrovia, Liberia, after suffering from a cerebral hemorrhage while serving as U.S. Ambassador to Liberia. Ambassador Locker was an attorney, public servant, politician, and diplomat who was also only the 2nd Black American to serve as U.S. Ambassador. He had been U.S. Ambassador to Liberia from 1953 until this untimely passing in 1955.

April 11

1974 On this day in 1975, Ambassador David Bolen presented his credentials to the leadership in Botswana, officially beginning his tenure in-residence as the leader of the U.S. Mission in this southern African country. While in Botswana, Bolen would simultaneously also serve as U.S. Ambassador to the nations of Lesotho and Swaziland from 1974 to 1976. He would also later be appointed as U.S. Ambassador to the German Democratic Republic, then popularly known as communist East Germany, from 1977 to 1980.

April 12

2021 On this day in 2021, the U.S. Secretary of State appointed Ambassador Gina Abercrombie-Winstanley as the Chief Diversity Officer of the U.S. Department of State. Ambassador Abercrombie-Winstanley was a career diplomat who had previously served as U.S. Ambassador to Malta from 2012 to 2016.

Major Milestone Moment

April 13

On this day in 2010, **Ambassador Mattie R. Sharpless** was interviewed by Stuart Kennedy of the Association for Diplomatic Studies and Training (ADST) as part of its Foreign Affairs Oral History Project. Ambassador Sharpless was an agricultural expert and career member of the Foreign Agricultural Service (FAS) of the U.S. Department of Agriculture (USDA). As a member of the FAS, she played a vital role in facilitating trade and international cooperation between other nations and the U.S., which helped ensure the continued vitality of the U.S. agricultural sector. Sharpless was the first Black American woman to be appointed from the ranks of the USDA/FAS to U.S. Ambassador.

April 14

1947 On this day in 1947, Pamela Bridgewater was born in Fredericksburg, Virginia. Bridgewater was a university educator and career diplomat who would serve as a U.S. Ambassador to three nations including Benin from 2000 to 2002; Ghana from 2005 to 2008; and Jamaica from 2010 to 2013.

April 15

2009 On this day in 2009, Bonnie Jenkins was nominated by President Barack Obama to be the Department of State's Coordinator of Threat Reduction Programs, with the rank of Ambassador. After Senate confirmation, she would serve in this role until 2017.

April 16

2003 On this day in 2003, Roland W. Bullen was appointed as U.S. Ambassador to Guyana. After Senate confirmation, he would serve in this role until 2006. While serving as Ambassador to Guyana, Bullen was also accredited as the first U.S. Plenipotentiary Representative to CARICOM (The Caribbean Community), which is a grouping of twenty countries, fifteen Member States, and five Associate Members in the region.

April 17

2013 On this day in 2013, the George Mason University student-run online news source *Connect2Mason* published a piece on the career of "U.S. Ambassador and George Mason Professor John M. Jones." Jones was an attorney, university educator, and career diplomat who served as U.S. Ambassador to Guyana from 2008 to 2009.

April 18

1961 On this day in 1961, Ambassador Clifton Wharton, Sr., presented his credentials to the leadership in Norway, officially beginning his tour as U.S. Ambassador to this European nation. Ambassador Wharton would be the first

Black American to serve as U.S. Ambassador to a European nation, doing so in Norway from 1961 to 1964. Earlier, Wharton would also be the first Black American to take and passed the U.S. Foreign Service Exam, becoming a Foreign Services Officer in 1925.

April 19
1982 On this day in 1982, Ambassador Howard Walker presented his credentials to the leadership in Togo, officially beginning his tenure in-residence as leader of the U.S. Mission in this African nation. Walker was a military veteran and career diplomat who served as U.S. Ambassador to Togo from 1982 to 1984, and then again later to Madagascar and the Comoros from 1989 to 1992.

April 20
1989 On this day in 1989, Ambassador Terence Todman was appointed to his 6th ambassadorial posting when President Ronald Reagan nominated him to be U.S. Ambassador to Argentina. After Senate confirmation, Ambassador Todman led the U.S. Mission as Ambassador in this South American nation from 1989 to 1993. Todman was a military veteran and career diplomat who has the distinction of being a U.S. Ambassador more than any other Black American in history (six total), including: to Chad from 1969 to 1972; to Guinea from 1972 to 1975; to Costa Rica from 1974 to 1977; to Spain from 1978 to 1983; to Denmark from 1983 to 1989; and, to Argentina from 1989 to 1993.

April 21
2014 On this day in 2014, Ambassador Ronald Palmer passed away. Ambassador Palmer was a career diplomat and university educator who would serve as a U.S. Ambassador on three occasions, including Togo from 1976 to 1978, Malaysia from 1981 to 1983, and Mauritius from 1986 to 1989.

April 22
1977 On this day in 1977, Ambassador Theodore Britton, Jr., officially ended his tenure as U.S. Ambassador to Barbados and Grenada, where he had served since 1974. Britton was a military veteran, public servant, and diplomat. While serving as U.S. Ambassador to Barbados and Grenada, he would also simultaneously serve as the U.S. Special Representative to the West Indian Island nations of Antigua, Dominica, St. Christopher, Nevis, Anguilla, St. Vincent, and St. Lucia.

April 23
1976 On this day in 1976, Ambassador William Carter presented his credentials to the leadership in Liberia, officially beginning his tenure in-residence as leader of the U.S. Mission to this African nation. Carter was a journalist and career diplomat who served as a U.S. Ambassador on three separate occasions: to Tanzania from 1972 to 1975, to Liberia from 1976 to 1979, and at-Large as Liaison with State and Local Government from 1979 to 1981.

April 24
2020 On this day in 2020, Ambassador Harry Thomas, Jr. was one of six former U.S. Ambassadors who participated in a high-level virtual dialogue moderated by former Secretary of State John Kerry. The event, virtually attended by more than 700 people, provided insights into the current state of U.S. diplomatic relations, which many argued had suffered tremendously under the Donald Trump administration. At the time, Ambassador Thomas was serving as a Kissinger Senior Fellow. He had previously served as U.S. Ambassador to Zimbabwe from 2016 to 2018, to the Philippines from 2010 to 2013, and to Bangladesh from 2003 to 2005.

April 25
1993 On this day in 1993, Ambassador Leonard Spearman, Sr. officially ended his term as U.S. Ambassador to Lesotho.

Spearman was a university educator and leader, public servant, and diplomat who served as U.S. Ambassador to Rwanda from 1988 to 1990 and to Lesotho from 1990 to 1993.

Major Milestone Moment

April 26

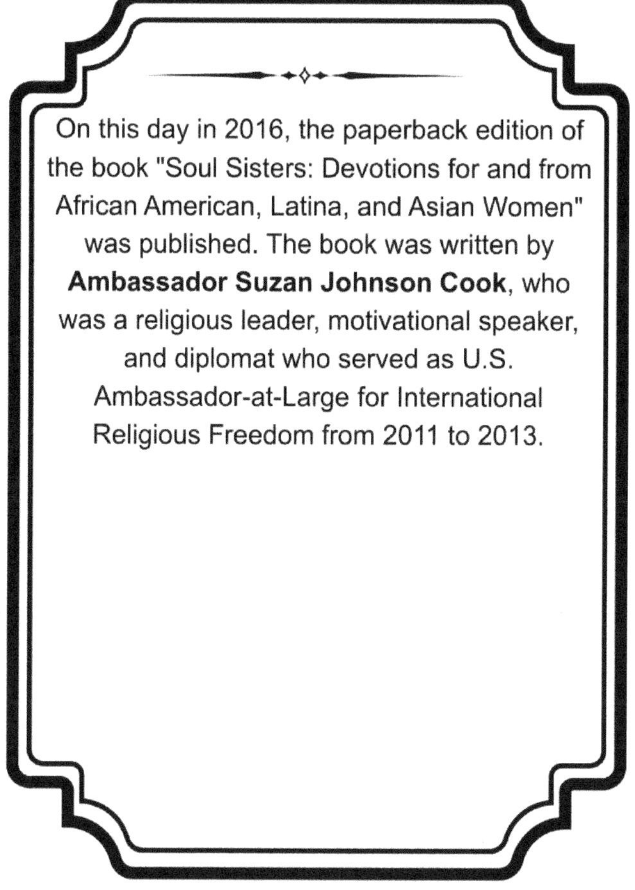

On this day in 2016, the paperback edition of the book "Soul Sisters: Devotions for and from African American, Latina, and Asian Women" was published. The book was written by **Ambassador Suzan Johnson Cook**, who was a religious leader, motivational speaker, and diplomat who served as U.S. Ambassador-at-Large for International Religious Freedom from 2011 to 2013.

April 27

2010 On this day in 2010, Ambassador Harry Thomas, Jr., presented his credentials to the leadership of the Philippines, officially beginning his tenure in-residence as leader of the U.S. diplomatic mission in this East Asia and Pacific Island nation. Thomas was a career diplomat who served as U.S. Ambassador on three separate occasions including Bangladesh from 2003 to 2005, the Philippines from 2010 to 2013, and Zimbabwe from 2016 to 2018.

April 28

1922 On this day in 1922, Jewel Stradford Lafontant was born in Chicago, Illinois. Lafontant would go on to serve as U.S. Coordinator for Refugee Affairs with the rank of Ambassador (Ambassador-at-Large) from 1989 to 1993.

April 29

2009 On this day in 2009, Ambassador Johnnie Carson testified before the U.S. Senate Foreign Relations Committee as President Barack Obama's nominee to become Assistant Secretary of State for African Affairs. Ambassador Carson was eventually confirmed by the U.S. Senate, and served in this role from 2009 to 2013. A career diplomat, he also served the U.S. as Ambassador on three separate occasions, including to Uganda from 1991 to 1994, Zimbabwe from 1995 to 1997, and Kenya from 1999 to 2003.

April 30

2007 On this day in 2007, President George W. Bush nominated Maurice C. Parker as U.S. Ambassador to Swaziland. Following Senate confirmation, Ambassador Parker served in this leadership role until 2009. Parker was a career diplomat who, in addition to this ambassadorial appointment, held several other leadership positions during his career, including as Director of Consular and International Programs at the Homeland Security Council in the Executive Office of the President.

2007 On this day in 2007, President George W. Bush nominated June Carter Perry to be the U.S. Ambassador to Sierra Leone. Following Senate confirmation, Ambassador Perry would serve in this leadership role until 2009. Previously, she had also served as U.S. Ambassador to Lesotho from 2004 to 2007.

CHAPTER 6:
MAY

May 1
2009 On this day in 2009, Beatrice W. Welters was announced as elected to the Board of Trustees of the Aspen Institute (a well-known nonprofit organization). The following year, President Barack Obama nominated Walters to be U.S. Ambassador to Trinidad & Tobago, where, after Senate confirmation, she served from May 2010 to November 2012.

May 2
1928 On this day in 1928, William B. Jones was born in Los Angeles, California. Jones was an attorney and career diplomat who would serve as U.S. Ambassador to Haiti from 1977 to 1980.

May 3
2022 On this day in 2023, Ambassador Linda Thomas-Greenfield, U.S. Permanent Representative to the United Nations (UN), delivered remarks on commemorating the 30th anniversary of World Freedom Day. She honored the memory of members of the press who had lost their lives doing their jobs and expressed that the United States would continue to advocate for press freedom worldwide.

May 4
2015 On this day in 2015, Ambassador Alfonso Lenhardt, who at the time was serving as Acting Administrator of the U.S. Agency for International Development (USAID), led a delegation of officials on a visit to Nepal to meet with government officials of that country and USAID partners, to survey and discuss the aftermath of the magnitude 7.8 earthquake that had hit Nepal several days earlier. Ambassador Lenhardt and his team joined Nepalese government officials on an aerial survey of the affected districts and observed the distribution of emergency relief supplies in the affected areas. Lenhardt was a military

veteran, public servant, and diplomat who had previously served as U.S. Ambassador to Tanzania from 2009 to 2013.

May 5

1918 On this day in 1981, Barbara Watson was born in New York, New York. Watson was a businesswoman, attorney, public servant, and diplomat who would serve as U.S. Ambassador to Malaysia from 1980 to 1981.

1908 On this day in 1908, Clinton Knox was born in New Bedford, Massachusetts. Knox was a military veteran, university educator, and career diplomat who served as U.S. Ambassador to the West African Republic of Dahomey (now called Benin) from 1964 to 1969, and later to Haiti from 1969 to 1973.

May 6

1949 On this day in 1949, America's first Black Ambassador, Edward R. Dudley, presented his credentials to the Liberian President, which officially marked the beginning of his historic ambassadorial tenure and laid the path for future Black Americans to be appointed as leaders of U.S. Missions abroad, with the rank and title of Ambassador.

May 7

1981 On this day in 1981, John Burroughs was nominated by President Ronald Reagan to be U.S. Ambassador to Malawi. After Senate confirmation, he would serve in this leadership role until 1984. He would later also serve as the U.S. Ambassador to Uganda from 1988 to 1991.

May 8

2006 On this day in 2006, the *American: The Jesuit Review* magazine published in its Faith in Focus issue an article entitled "From Grief to Hope." In it, the author reflects on the early stages of Loyola Jesuit College which was being planned in Abuja, Nigeria, back in 1995. He highlights how, as Ambassador Walter Carrington, who was then serving as

U.S. Ambassador to that African nation, "surveyed the terrain, he uttered powerful and prophetic words..." speaking...of a 'field of dreams,' imagining what a wonderful educational institution would soon be in place. According to the author, "he [Ambassador Carrington] was familiar with Jesuit education and knew that Loyola Jesuit College could become a center of excellence in secondary education. Carrington was a military veteran, attorney, scholar, and diplomat who served as U.S. Ambassador to Senegal from 1980 to 1981 and then to Nigeria from 1993 to 1997.

May 9
1994 On this day in 1994, Irving Hicks, Sr., was nominated by President Bill Clinton, to be U.S. Ambassador to Ethiopia. After Senate confirmation, Ambassador Hick served in this role until 1996. Hicks was a career diplomat who served as U.S. Ambassador on three separate occasions including to the Seychelles from 1985 to 1987, the United Nation's Security Council with the rank of Ambassador from 1992 to 1993, and Ethiopia from 1994 to 1996.

May 10
2021 On this day in 2021, Ambassador Bonnie Jenkins and Ambassador Gina Abercrombie-Winstanley were officially announced by the online website *Travel Noire* as guests on the first season of the new Black Professionals in International Affairs' podcast called *Global Take*. The podcast focused on sharing unique perspectives from Black leaders on the most pressing global issues, examining how these challenges affect communities both at home and abroad.

2012 On this day in 2012, Ambassador Bonnie Jenkins, in her role as State Department Coordinator for Threat Reduction Programs, spoke on the topic of "The G-8 Global Partnership Against the Spread of WMD: A Case Study of Summit-Sponsored Initiatives" at Northwestern University.

May 11

1899 On this day in 1899, Clifton Wharton, Sr., was born in Baltimore, Maryland. Wharton was an attorney and career diplomat who served as U.S. Ambassador to Norway from 1961 to 1964, making him the first Black American to serve as a U.S. Ambassador in a European country. Wharton, Sr., was also the first Black American to pass the State Department's Foreign Service Exam, doing so in 1925.

Major Milestone Moment

May 12

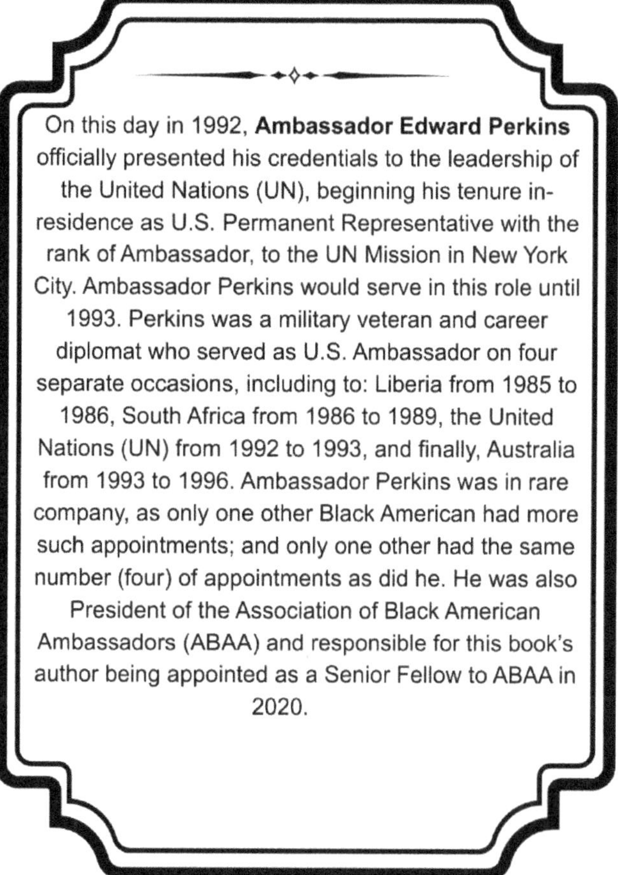

On this day in 1992, **Ambassador Edward Perkins** officially presented his credentials to the leadership of the United Nations (UN), beginning his tenure in-residence as U.S. Permanent Representative with the rank of Ambassador, to the UN Mission in New York City. Ambassador Perkins would serve in this role until 1993. Perkins was a military veteran and career diplomat who served as U.S. Ambassador on four separate occasions, including to: Liberia from 1985 to 1986, South Africa from 1986 to 1989, the United Nations (UN) from 1992 to 1993, and finally, Australia from 1993 to 1996. Ambassador Perkins was in rare company, as only one other Black American had more such appointments; and only one other had the same number (four) of appointments as did he. He was also President of the Association of Black American Ambassadors (ABAA) and responsible for this book's author being appointed as a Senior Fellow to ABAA in 2020.

May 13

2009 On this day in 2009, Ambassador Barry Wells officially ended his tenure as U.S. Ambassador to The Gambia, where he had served since 2008. Wells was a university educator and diplomat who had served as U.S. Ambassador to The Gambia since 2008. In addition to this role, he had also held several other key leadership positions, including appointments by Secretary of State Condoleezza Rice as Director of the State Department's Office of Civil Rights in 2006, then as its Chief Diversity Officer in 2007.

May 14

2015 On this day in 2015, John L. Estrada was nominated by President Barack Obama as U.S. Ambassador to Trinidad & Tobago. Following his Senate confirmation in 2016, he would serve in this role until 2017. In addition to his diplomatic leadership as a U.S. Ambassador, Estrada was also a military veteran who had enlisted in the U.S. Marine Corps in 1973, and spent 34 years in the Corps, eventually rising to serve in its highest-ranking enlisted position – Sergeant Major.

May 15

2011 On this day in 2011, Suzan Johnson Cook officially began her tenure as U.S. Ambassador-at-Large for International Religious Freedom. She would serve in this leadership role until 2013. Cook was a religious leader, motivational speaker, and diplomat who, in addition to her service as Ambassador-at-Large for International Religious Freedom, had earlier been the first female and 1st Black American to serve as the Chaplain of the New York City Police Department's (NYPD) (1990).

May 16

2011 On this day in 2011, Ambassador Clyde Bishop served as the keynote speaker for the annual Salvation Army Civic Dinner at the Chase Center on the Riverfront in Wilmington, Delaware. Ambassador Bishop was a Delaware State

University and a University of Delaware Alumnus who went on to become a university educator and career diplomat. He would also serve as U.S. Ambassador to the Marshall Islands from 2006 to 2008.

Major Milestone Moment

May 17

On this day in 1983, **Arthur Lewis** was nominated by President Ronald Reagan to be U.S. Ambassador to Sierra Leone. After Senate confirmation, Ambassador Lewis would serve in this role until 1986. Lewis was a military veteran and diplomat who, prior to his service as U.S. Ambassador to Sierra Leone, had a diplomatic career marked by efforts to increase the diversity of the U.S. diplomatic establishment. For example, he enlisted the support of the Ford Foundation to create an expanded minority recruitment program for the U.S. Information Agency (USIA) in 1967. The program targeted ethnic minorities in universities around the nation, and brought students to Washington, DC, for expanded training in history, language, and international affairs as preparation for successfully completing the Foreign Services entrance exam.

May 18

2017 On this day in 2017, Tulinabo S. Mushingi was confirmed by the U.S. Senate as U.S. Ambassador to Senegal and concurrently to Guinea-Bissau following his nomination by the President to this role. Mushingi would be one of only five (5) Black Americans appointed by the 45th President during his first administration. Ambassador Mushingi was a career diplomat who served as the U.S. Ambassador to Burkina Faso from 2013 to 2016, Senegal and concurrently Guinea-Bissau from 2017 to 2021, and Angola and São Tomé and Principe from 2021 to 2025.

May 19

2011 On this day in 2011, Ambassador Teddy Taylor (at the U.S. Embassy in Papua New Guinea) presented the Secretary of State's International Women of Courage Award to a rural businesswoman, Betty Maria Higgins, for her contributions to the local business culture and for her work mentoring young women. Taylor was a career diplomat who served as U.S. Ambassador to several Pacific Island nations concurrently, including Papua New Guinea, Solomon Islands, and Vanuatu from 2009 to 2012.

May 20

2013 On this day in 2013, Ambassador Susan Rice was the focus of an article entitled "Rice on Counterterrorism" in a Voice of American (VOA) report. In this report, the VOA discussed how Rice had previously outlined U.S. priorities to reduce terrorism in Africa through intensifying capacity-building assistance to African partners. At the time, Rice was serving as U.S. Permanent Representative to the United Nations with the Rank of Ambassador.

May 21

1991 On this day in 1991, Ambassador George Moose ended his tenure as U.S. Ambassador to Senegal, where he had served since 1988. He had also previously served as U.S. Ambassador to Benin from 1983 to 1986 and would later serve as the U.S. Permanent Representative to the European Office of the United Nations (UN) in Geneva with the rank of Ambassador from 1997 to 2001.

May 22

1989 On this day in 1989, Ambassador Edward Perkins officially ended his tenure as U.S. Ambassador to South Africa, where he had served since 1986. Perkins was a military veteran and career diplomat who served as U.S. Ambassador on four separate occasions, including to Liberia from 1985 to 1986, to South Africa from 1986 to 1989, to the United Nations (UN) from 1992 to 1993, and to Australia from 1993 to 1996. Perkins would also later become President of the Association of Black American Ambassadors (ABAA).

May 23

2022 On this day in 2022, Ambassador Linda Thomas-Greenfield delivered remarks at a UN Security Council Briefing on Somalia. Her remarks focused on the Security Council's recent elections, the terrorist threat from al-Shabaab, and the dire humanitarian and economic crises facing Somalia at that time. Thomas-Greenfield was a university educator and career diplomat who had served as U.S. Ambassador to Liberia from 2008 to 2012, before taking over leadership of the U.S. Mission to the United Nations in New York from 2021 to 2025.

May 24

2011 On this day in 2011, Ambassador Pamela L. Spratlen presented her credentials to the leadership of the Kyrgyz Republic, officially beginning her tenure in-residence as the leader of the U.S. Mission to this Eurasian nation. Spratlen was a career diplomat who served as U.S. Ambassador to the Kyrgyz Republic from 2011 to 2014 and then again to Uzbekistan from 2015 to 2018.

May 25

2004 On this day in 2004, Jendayi Frazer was nominated by President George W. Bush to be U.S. Ambassador to South Africa. After Senate confirmation, she would become the first ever woman to serve in this leadership position in this key Southern African nation. Frazer was a university educator, scholar, and diplomat who, in addition to her service as U.S. Ambassador to South Africa from 2004 to 2005, served in several other key public service roles including as Assistant Secretary of State in the Bureau of African Affairs from 2005 to 2009.

May 26

1996 On this day in 1996, Ambassador Irving Hicks, Sr., officially ended his tenure as U.S. Ambassador in Ethiopia, where he had served since 1994. Hicks was a career diplomat who had previously served as U.S. Ambassador to the Seychelles from 1985 to 1987 and to the United Nations' Security Council with the rank of Ambassador from 1992 to 1993, before his 1994 to 1996 ambassadorial role in Ethiopia.

May 27

2003 On this day in 2003, Harry K. Thomas, Jr., was nominated by President George W. Bush to be U.S. Ambassador to Bangladesh. After Senate confirmation, he would serve in this role until 2005. Thomas was a career diplomat who, in addition to his service as U.S. Ambassador to Bangladesh from 2003 to 2005, later served as U.S. Ambassador to the Philippines from 2010 to 2013, and then to Zimbabwe from 2016 to 2018.

Major Milestone Moment

May 28

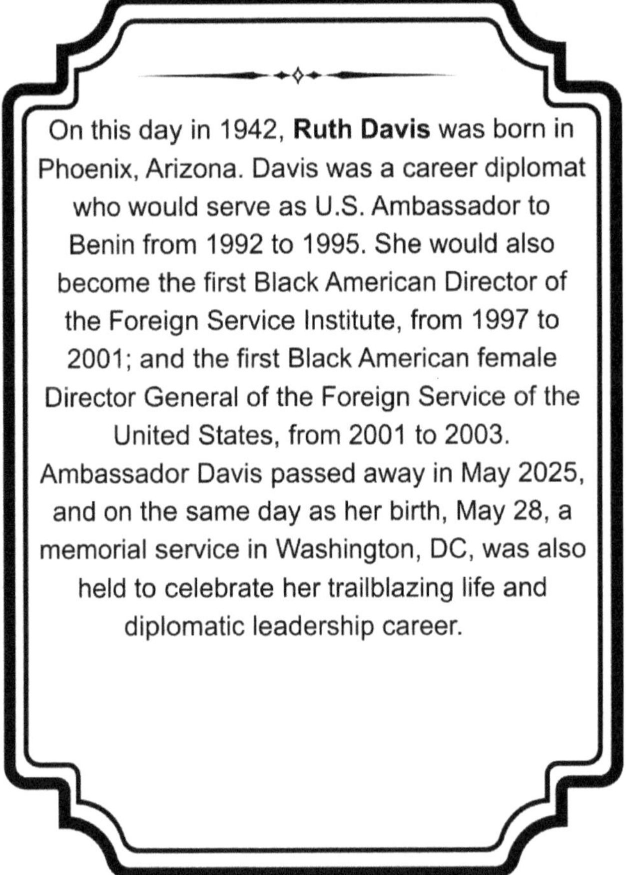

On this day in 1942, **Ruth Davis** was born in Phoenix, Arizona. Davis was a career diplomat who would serve as U.S. Ambassador to Benin from 1992 to 1995. She would also become the first Black American Director of the Foreign Service Institute, from 1997 to 2001; and the first Black American female Director General of the Foreign Service of the United States, from 2001 to 2003. Ambassador Davis passed away in May 2025, and on the same day as her birth, May 28, a memorial service in Washington, DC, was also held to celebrate her trailblazing life and diplomatic leadership career.

May 29

2009 On this day in 2009, Ambassador Ronald Kirk, the newly appointed U.S. Trade Representative, was the subject of an online article in the *The New York Times* entitled "Trade Diplomat Taps His Deal-Making Past." Kirk had previously served as Mayor of Dallas, Texas, and was now embarking on his new role as U.S. Trade Representative, with the rank of Ambassador. He would serve in that role from 2009 to 2013.

May 30

2002 On this day in 2002, Ambassador Pierre-Richard Prosper, who was serving as U.S. Ambassador-at-Large for War Crimes, was quoted on multiple occasions in a *Washington Post* article entitled "White House Wants Trial Kickbacks Ended." He focused on how the Bush administration was pressuring the United Nations (UN) to "crack down harder on kickbacks paid to war-crimes suspects by their U.N.-financed defense lawyers at international tribunals for the former Yugoslavia and Rwanda." Prosper was an attorney and diplomat who served as U.S. Ambassador-at-Large for War Crimes from 2001 to 2005.

2025 On this day in 2025, Ambassador Brenda Schoonover recorded a brief interview with *Fearrington StoryCorps* about her life and career. Including in her remarks, Ambassador Schoonover made certain to highlight how she was among the nine Black students who had integrated Catonsville High School in Maryland in her youth. Also, she later became a member of the inaugural class of the U.S. Peace Corps volunteers in 1961. Ambassador Schoonover was a career diplomat who served as U.S. Ambassador to Togo from 1997 to 2000.

May 31

1924 On this day in 1924, Patricia Roberts-Harris was born in Mattoon, Illinois. Roberts-Harris was an attorney, public servant, and diplomat, who would become the first Black American woman to ever serve as a U.S. Ambassador, serving as such to Luxembourg from 1965 to 1967. She was later appointed as the Dean of the Howard University School of Law (1969), the school's first female Dean. She also served as U.S. Secretary of Housing and Urban Development (1977), making her the first Black American woman to ever hold a Cabinet-level post, and the first to ever be part of the Presidential Line of Succession.

1891 On this day in 1891, Jessie D. Locker was born in College Hill (Cincinnati), Ohio. Locker was an attorney, public servant, politician, and diplomat who would become only the second Black American ever to be appointed and serve as U.S. Ambassador. He served as U.S. Ambassador to Liberia from 1953 to 1955.

1997 On this day in 1997, Ambassador Jewel Stradford Lafontant passed away from breast cancer. Lafontant was an attorney, public servant, and diplomat who would serve as U.S. Coordinator for Refugee Affairs, with the rank of Ambassador-at-Large from 1989 to 1993. She had also been the first Black American woman to serve as an Assistant U.S. Attorney and the first to have argued a case before the U.S. Supreme Court.

CHAPTER 7:
JUNE

June 1
2007 On this day in 2007, Ambassador James McGee officially ended his tenure as U.S. Ambassador to both Madagascar and The Comoros, where he had served simultaneously since 2004. McGee was a military veteran and career diplomat who served as U.S. Ambassador to Swaziland from 2002 to 2004, prior to his service as Ambassador to Madagascar and concurrently to the Indian Ocean Island nation of The Comoros from 2004 to 2007. He would later also serve as U.S. Ambassador to Zimbabwe from 2007 to 2009.

June 2
1941 On this day in 1941, Anne Forrester Holloway was born in Philadelphia, Pennsylvania. Forrester Holloway was a scholar, activist, university educator, and diplomat who would serve as U.S. Ambassador to Mali from 1979 to 1981.

June 3
1956 On this day in 1956, Harry Thomas, Jr., was born in New York (Harlem), New York. Thomas was a career diplomat who served as U.S. Ambassador to Bangladesh from 2003 to 2005, the Philippines from 2010 to 2013, and Zimbabwe from 2016 to 2018.

June 4
1965 On this day in 1965, Patricia Roberts Harris was nominated by President Lyndon Johnson to be U.S. Ambassador to Luxembourg. After Senate confirmation, she would become the first Black American female to be a U.S. Ambassador, serving as such in Luxembourg until 1967.

June 5
1986 On this day in 1986, Ambassador Arthur Lewis officially ended his tenure as U.S. Ambassador to Sierra

Leone. Lewis was a military veteran and diplomat who served as Ambassador to Sierra Leone since 1983. During his career, Lewis was instrumental in establishing several programs within the U.S. Information Agency (USIA) to expand opportunities for minorities within this U.S. government agency, which is responsible for promoting American culture and values abroad.

2025 On this day in 2025, Ambassador Ervin Massinga was quoted by the Ethiopian news agency Horn Diplomat as he voiced U.S. support for the landlocked country of Ethiopia's efforts to secure maritime access through diplomatic and peaceful means. Specifically, Ambassador Massinga is quoted as saying that "strengthening maritime access through commercial, diplomatic, and peaceful avenues is a fundamental priority — one that the United States government and my embassy are fully committed to supporting." Ambassador Massinga was a career diplomat who had begun serving as U.S. Ambassador to Ethiopia in 2023 and was still leading the U.S. Mission in this African nation at the time of writing in 2025.

June 6

2022 On this day in 2022, Ambassador Sharon Cromer received and welcomed the new cohort of U.S. Peace Corps volunteers who returned to The Gambia for the first time after a two-year-long Peace Corps volunteer break caused by the COVID-19 pandemic. Ambassador Cromer, an international development specialist and career diplomat in the U.S. Agency for International Development (USAID), served as U.S. Ambassador to The Gambia from 2022 to 2025.

June 7

1929 and 1944 On this day in 1929, Gerald Thomas was born in Natick, Massachusetts and on this day in 1944, George Moose was born in New York, New York. Thomas was a military veteran, a career military officer, university educator, and a diplomat who served as U.S. Ambassador to the South American nation of Guyana from 1981 to 1983, and to Kenya from 1983 to 1989.

Moose was a career diplomat who served as U.S. Ambassador to Benin from 1983 to 1986, to Senegal from 1988 to 1991, and as the U.S. Permanent Representative to the European Office of the United Nations (UN) in Geneva, with the rank of Ambassador from 1997 to 2001. He was also one of only 5 Black Americans in our nation's history, to ever earn the rank of Career Ambassador (2002). This book's author, born on this day in 1974, is honored to share a birthday with these distinguished Black leaders.

Major Milestone Moment

June 7

On this day in 2006, **Ambassador Jendayi Frazer** and **Ambassador Cindy Courville** were among the American leaders praised for their efforts in leading U.S. support for the African Growth and Opportunity Act (AGOA). Specifically, the two were highlighted in *The Perspective* online news' report on the AGOA forum held in Washington, DC, where U.S. and African leaders met to discuss the progress and future of this legislation intended to increase trade between the U.S. and African nations. At the time, Dr. Frazer and Dr. Courville, were serving as Assistant U.S. Secretary of State for African Affairs and Senior Director for African Affairs at the National Security Council (NSC), respectively. Dr. Frazer had previously served as U.S. Ambassador to South Africa from 2004 to 2005, while Dr. Courville would later serve as U.S. Ambassador to the African Union from 2006 to 2008.

June 8

1931 On this day in 1931, Ulric Haynes, Jr. was born in New York (Brooklyn), New York. Haynes was a public and private sector servant, diplomat, and university leader who would serve as U.S. Ambassador to Algeria from 1977 to 1981. During this time, in November of 1979, while Haynes was U.S. Ambassador to Algeria, the Iran Hostage Crisis occurred, where 66 hostages were held at the American Embassy in Tehran, Iran. Because of his previous experiences in Tehran and his familiarity with the region, he was able to play a key role in negotiating the release of the hostages.

June 9

2007 On this day in 2007, Ambassador Roger Pierce officially ended his tenure as U.S. Ambassador to Cape Verde, where he had served since 2005. Pierce was a career diplomat who shortly after his service as U.S. Ambassador to Cape Verde, retired from formal governmental service. He joined the Office of Career Services at the University of New Mexico in Albuquerque disseminating information and identifying and counseling candidates for the U.S. Foreign Service.

June 10

1998 On this day in 1998, Ambassador Bismarck Myrick officially ended his tenure as U.S. Ambassador to Lesotho, where he had served since 1995. Myrick was a military veteran and career diplomat who, in addition to serving as Ambassador to Lesotho, would later also serve as U.S. Ambassador to Liberia from 1999 to 2002.

June 11

1999 On this day in 1999, Ambassador Leslie Alexander officially ended his tenure as U.S. Ambassador to Ecuador, where he had served since 1996. Alexander was a career diplomat who, in addition to having served as U.S.

Ambassador to Mauritius and Comoros, he would later also serve as U.S. Ambassador to Ecuador from 1996 to 1999.

June 12
2009 On this day in 2009, Ambassador Maurice Parker officially ended his tenure as U.S. Ambassador to Swaziland, where he had served since 2007. Parker was a career diplomat who, in addition to this leadership role within the U.S. diplomatic establishment, had also served as Director of the Foreign Service Assignments Division in the State Department and as Director of the Office of Employee Relations in the same Bureau.

June 13
1989 On this day in 1989, Ambassador Terence Todman presented his credentials to the leadership in Argentina, officially beginning his tenure in-residence as the leader of the U.S. diplomatic Mission in this South American nation. This would be the final of his six total U.S. ambassadorial appointments (more than any other Black American at the time of writing). The other appointments included: Chad from 1969 to 1972; Guinea from 1982 to 1975; Costa Rica from 1975 to 1977; Spain from 1978 to 1983, and Denmark from 1983 to 1989.

June 14
1999 On this day in 1999, President Bill Clinton nominated Bismarck Myrick to be U.S. Ambassador to Liberia. Following Senate confirmation, he would take up this role as U.S. Ambassador and serve in Liberia until 2002. Myrick was a military veteran and career diplomat who, in addition to serving as Ambassador to Liberia, had previously also served as U.S. Ambassador to Lesotho from 1995 to 1998.

June 15
1953 On this day in 1953, Edward Dudley, America's first Black Ambassador, departs his post in Liberia, where he had served as U.S. Ambassador since 1949, and returned to his

legal career in the United States. Dudley was an attorney, civil rights advocate, judge, and diplomat who in addition to holding the distinction of being the country's first Black American U.S. Ambassador he also worked with future Supreme Court Justice–and America's first Black Supreme Court Justice – Thurgood Marshall. They worked on many landmark civil rights cases during both their tenures at the National Association for the Advancement of Colored People (NAACP).

June 16

1992 On this day in 1992, President Bill Clinton nominated Irving Hicks, Sr., to be Alternate Representative of the U.S.A. to the 47th Session of the General Assembly of the United Nations, with the rank of Ambassador. Hicks was a career diplomat who held three ambassadorial appointments during his career, including: U.S. Ambassador to the Seychelles from 1985 to 1987, the United Nations' Security Council with the rank of Ambassador from 1992 to 1993, and Ethiopia from 1994 to 1996.

June 17

2009 On this day in 2009, the news outlet, *Politico,* reported that President Barack Obama planned to nominate William Kennard as the next U.S. Representative to the European Union (EU). Kennard was an attorney and telecommunications expert who previously served as Chairman of the Federal Communications Commission (FCC). The reporting was correct as President Obama officially made that nomination, and after Senate confirmation in November of 2009, Ambassador Kennard would serve as the U.S. leader of its EU diplomatic mission until 2013.

June 18

2015 On this day in 2015, President Barack Obama nominated Gentry O. Smith to be Director of the Office of Foreign Missions at the U.S. Department of State, with the rank of Ambassador. After Senate Confirmation, Ambassador Smith served in this role until 2017. Smith was a former law enforcement officer as well as a global security expert and diplomat.

June 19

1974 On this day in 1974, Ambassador Clarence Clyde Ferguson delivered a speech on behalf of the United States to the Ad Hoc Committee on Special Programs of the United Nations (UN) Economic and Social Council. This statement was made in his capacity as the U.S. Representative to the UN Council. Ferguson was a military veteran, attorney, and diplomat who had previously served as U.S. Ambassador to Uganda from 1970 to 1972.

June 20

1924 On this day in 1924, Elliott Skinner was born in Port of Spain, Trinidad and Tobago. Skinner was a military veteran, anthropologist, university educator, and diplomat who served as U.S. Ambassador to Upper Volta (now called Burkina Faso) from 1966 to 1969.

1947 On this day in 1947, Gayleatha Brown was born in Matawan, West Virginia. Brown was a career diplomat who served as U.S. Ambassador to Benin from 2006 to 2009. She was also appointed and confirmed as U.S. Ambassador to Burkina Faso (2009), but was not able to serve in this posting.

June 21

1927 On this day in 1927, Carl Stokes was born in Cleveland, Ohio. Stokes was a military veteran, attorney, public servant, and diplomat who would serve as U.S. Ambassador to the Seychelles from 1994 to 1995.

June 22

2001 On this day in 2001, Ambassador Delano Lewis officially ended his tenure as U.S. Ambassador to South

Africa. Lewis was an attorney, businessman, and diplomat who served as U.S. Ambassador to South Africa from 1999 until his departure in 2001. Prior to his role leading the U.S. Mission in South Africa, Lewis had held many leadership positions, including as the President and CEO of National Public Radio (NPR), the first Black American to ever hold that position.

Major Milestone Moment

June 23

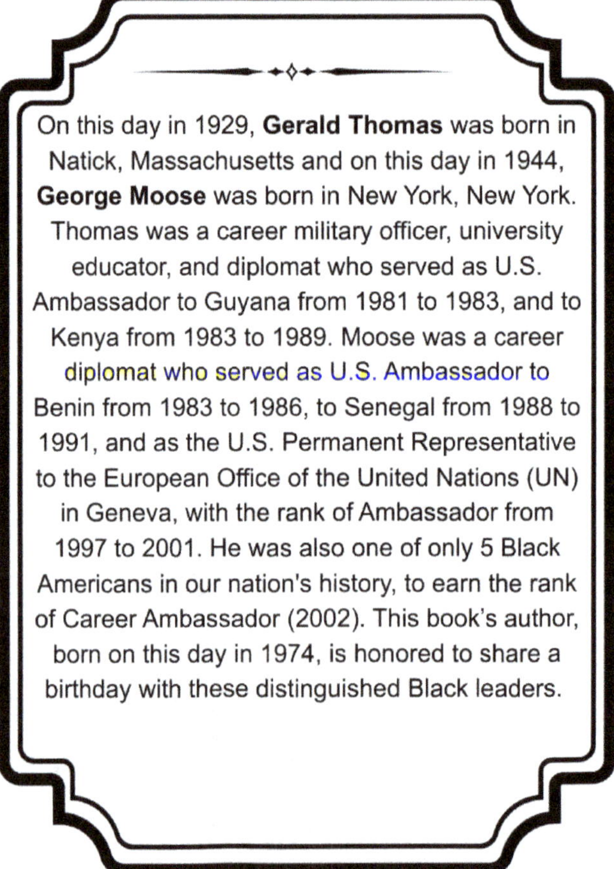

On this day in 1929, **Gerald Thomas** was born in Natick, Massachusetts and on this day in 1944, **George Moose** was born in New York, New York. Thomas was a career military officer, university educator, and diplomat who served as U.S. Ambassador to Guyana from 1981 to 1983, and to Kenya from 1983 to 1989. Moose was a career diplomat who served as U.S. Ambassador to Benin from 1983 to 1986, to Senegal from 1988 to 1991, and as the U.S. Permanent Representative to the European Office of the United Nations (UN) in Geneva, with the rank of Ambassador from 1997 to 2001. He was also one of only 5 Black Americans in our nation's history, to earn the rank of Career Ambassador (2002). This book's author, born on this day in 1974, is honored to share a birthday with these distinguished Black leaders.

June 23

1944 On this day in 1944, George Moose was born in New York, New York. Moose was a career diplomat who served as U.S. Ambassador to Benin from 1983 to 1986, to Senegal from 1988 to 1991, and as the U.S. Permanent Representative to the European Office of the United Nations (UN) in Geneva, with the rank of Ambassador from 1997 to 2001. He was also one of only 5 Black Americans in our nation's history, to ever earn the rank of Career Ambassador (2002).

June 24

1955 On this day in 1955, Ambassador Richard Jones presented his credentials to the leadership of Liberia, officially beginning his tenure in-residence as leader of the U.S. Mission in this West African nation. Jones was a military veteran and leader, and only the third ever Black American to serve as a U.S. Ambassador. He would do so in Liberia until 1959.

June 25

2025 On this day in 2025, Ambassador Ervin Massinga was quoted by the Ethiopian news agency Horn Diplomat as he voiced U.S. support for the landlocked country of Ethiopia's efforts to secure maritime access through diplomatic and peaceful means. Specifically, Ambassador Massinga is quoted as saying that "strengthening maritime access through commercial, diplomatic, and peaceful avenues is a fundamental priority — one that the United States government and my embassy are fully committed to supporting." Ambassador Massinga was a career diplomat who had begun serving as U.S. Ambassador to Ethiopia in 2023 and was still leading the U.S. Mission in this African nation at the time of writing in 2025.

June 26

2011 On this day in 2011, Ambassador Pamela Spratlen was the subject of an article published by the online media site *AllGov*. The article was titled "Ambassador to Kyrgyzstan: Who Is Pamela Spratlen?" It provided biographic information about the newly confirmed U.S. Ambassador to Kyrgyzstan (the Kyrgyz Republic) and highlighted some of her career accomplishments. Among those career highlights were some of her early public service activities, including her work at Volunteers in Service to America (VISTA) in California. Ambassador Spratlen was a career diplomat who would serve as U.S. Ambassador to that country from 2011 to 2014, and then later as U.S. Ambassador to Uzbekistan from 2015 to 2018.

June 27

1954 On this day in 1954, Ronald Kirk was born in Austin, Texas. Kirk was an attorney, public servant, and diplomat who served as the U.S. Trade Representative with the rank of Ambassador from 2009 to 2013. He would be the first Black American to ever serve as U.S. Trade Representative. Earlier in his career, Kirk had also served as Mayor of the City of Dallas, Texas (1992-2002), the first Black American to lead that major U.S. city.

June 28

1951 On this day in 1951, C. Steven McGann was born in New York, New York. McGann was a career diplomat who served as U.S. Ambassador concurrently to five Pacific Island nations, including Fiji, Kiribati, Nauru, Tonga, and Tuvalu from 2009 to 2011.

June 29

1998 On this day in 1998, Charles R. Stith, according to the State Department Office of the Historian, was appointed as U.S. Ambassador to Tanzania. After U.S. Senate confirmation, he would serve in this role until 2001. Stith was a minister, university educator and administrator, and diplomat. As U.S. Ambassador to Tanzania, he led the revitalization of the U.S. Mission there following the 1998 bombing on the Embassy by Al Qaeda, which killed 22 Americans and Tanzanians.

June 30

1999 On this day in 1999, Ambassador Arlene Render officially ended her tenure as U.S. Ambassador to Zambia, where she had served since 1996. Render was a career diplomat who served as U.S. Ambassador on three separate occasions, including to The Gambia from 1990 to 1993, to Zambia from 1996 to 1999, and to Côte d'Ivoire from 2001 to 2004.

Ambassador Edward Dudley. America's First Black Ambassador. Source: Edward R. Dudley papers, Amistad Research Center, New Orleans, LA

Ambassador Jerome Holland (#86), in his early life, prior to his ambassadorship, with his fellow varsity football team members at Cornell University in 1935. Source: Aggregated Cornell Photographs, #13-6-2957. Division of Rare and Manuscript Collections, Cornell University Library.

Ambassador Eunice Reddick visits the University of Diffa, Niger in 2017 Source: Amb Reddick

Ambassador Jerome Holland at the White House with President Richard Nixon and Secretary of State Henry Kissinger in 1970. Source: Jerome H. Holland papers, #2-10-2727. Division of Rare and Manuscript Collections, Cornell University Library

Ambassador Clinton Knox and his family.
Source: Knox Family papers, Amistad Research Center, New Orleans, LA

Ambassador Eunice Reddick (standing to right) at Orphanage in Niamey, Niger in 2017. Source: Amb Reddick

Colin L. Powell, Secretary, U. S. Department of State, launching Mattie Sharpless off as Ambassador to the Central African Republic, October 2001. Source: Amb Sharpless

Ambassador June Carter Perry with Dr. John Hope at a Thursday Luncheon Group (TLG) event. Source: Amb Perry

Ambassador Eunice Reddick (4th from the left) at Grand Mosque in Agadez, Niger with the Sultanate of Agadez officials, U.S. Embassy staff and American officials. Source: Amb Reddick

US-Namibian Partnership

Director General of the National Planning Commission, Tom Alweendo, and the American Ambassador to Namibia, Dennise Mathieu, exchange files after signing the HIV/AIDS partnership framework agreement. The framework is a five-year co-operation developed by the Republic of Namibia and the Government of the United States of America, to further support the development and implementation of the national response to HIV/AIDS in Namibia. It will also focus on sustainability, system strengthening and capacity development in the national HIV/AIDS response to improve health and healthcare for all Namibians.

Ambassador Dennise Mathieu and Tom Alweedo, Director General of the Namibian National Planning Commission, sign the HIV/AIDS partnership framework agreement. Source: Amb Mathieu

Ambassador Steve McGann and Dr. Carlton McLellan (Author) with students from Lima, Ohio during their visit to Washington, DC in April 2023. Source: Author

Ambassador Mchael Battle with Vice President Kamala Harris. Source: Amb Battle

President George W. Bush launching Mattie Sharpless off as U.S. Ambassador to the Central African Republic, from The White House, October 2001. Source: Amb Sharpless

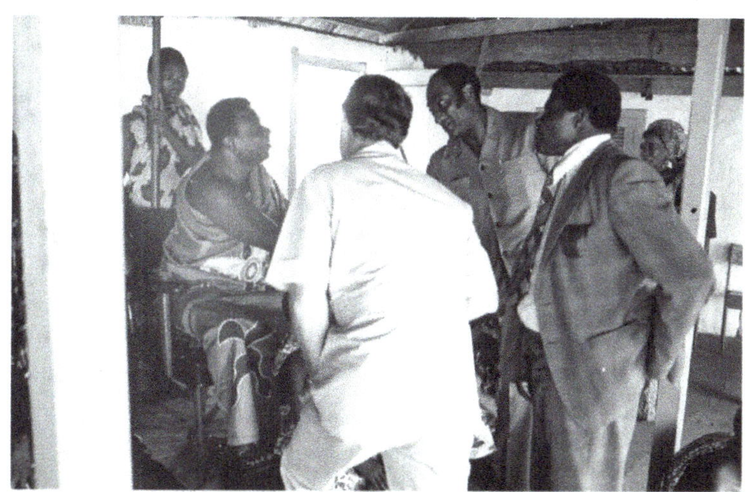

U.S. Embassy Accra Political Counselor Edward Perkins (future U.S. Ambassador), second from right, engages with a tribal chief in Ghana in 1978. Source: Courtesy of the Perkins family, from "Pioneer, Bridge Builder and Statesman—A Conversation with Ambassador Edward J. Perkins," published in The Foreign Service Journal, December 2020, Ambassador June Carter Perry (center) with Lesoth King Letsie III and Queen Masenate Mohato Seeiso (seated) and others. Source: Amb Perry. Republished with permission.

Ambassador Edward Perkins and U.N. Secretary-General Kofi Annan meet on March 15, 1999. Source: Photo courtesy of the Perkins family, from "Pioneer, Bridge Builder and Statesman—A Conversation with Ambassador Edward J. Perkins," published in The Foreign Service Journal, December 2020, https://afsa.org/pioneer-bridge-builder-and-statesman-conversation-ambassador-edward-j-perkins. Republished with permission.

Ambassador June Carter Perry (center) with Lesoth King Letsie III and Queen Masenate Mohato Seeiso (seated) and others. Source: Amb Perry

Ambassador Mattie R. Sharpless Highway, designated on May 10, 2018, in her home town, Hampstead/Surf City, North Carolina. Source: Amb Sharpless

Ambassador Charles Ray participating in a personnel recovery exercise during his tenure as Deputy Assistant Secretary of Defense for POW/Missing Personnel Affairs (2006-2009). Source: Amb Ray

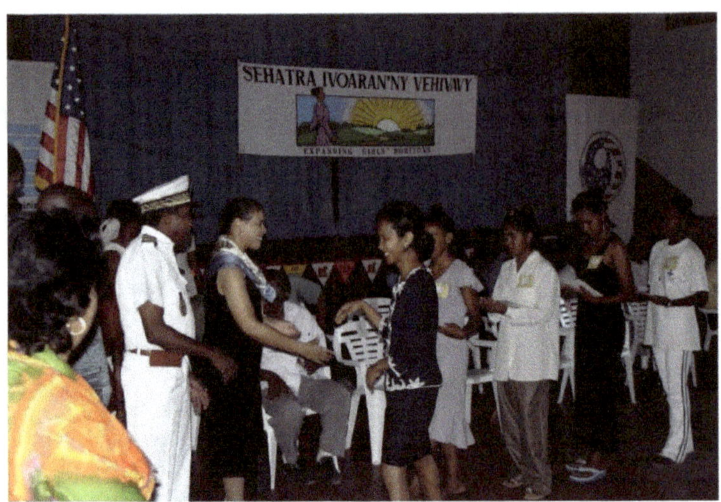

Ambassador Wanda Nesbitt presenting certificates to school girls chosen to receive an Ambassadors' Girls Scholarship in Madagascar. Source: Amb Nesbitt

Ambassador Charles Ray (center, facing camera), early in his career, prior to his first ambassadorship, served as Consul at the U.S. Consulate General in Chiang Mai, Thailand (1988-1991). Here he is working with the Thai government on anti-narcotics programs. Source: Amb Ray

Ambassador Dennise Mathieu swearing in by Secretary of State Colin Powell in 2002. Source: Amb Mathieu

Ambassador Michael Battle with Tanzanian President Samia Suluhu Hassan: Source: Amb Battle

Ambassador Steve McGann and Smith sisters from from Lima, Ohio during their visit to Washington, DC in April 2023. Source: Author

Ambassador Steve with Ann and Larry Miles from Lima, Ohio during their visit students to Washington, DC in April 2023. Source: Author

Ambassador Mchael Battle with President Barack Obama.
Source: Amb Battle

Ambassador Wanda Nesbitt (2nd from left) with President of Madagascar Marc Ravaolomana and various local and American businessmen at a ribbon cutting in 2003.
Source: Amb Nesbitt

Ambassador Todd Robinson with Dr. Carlton McLellan (Author) at the State Department in May 2023. Source: Author

Ambassador Charles Ray being presented his retirement certificate from Ambassador Linda Thomas-Greenfield during her tenure as Director General, in 2012. Source: Amb Ray

Ambassador Edward Perkins talks with President Ronald Reagan and others in the Oval Office. Source: Courtesy of the Perkins family, from "Pioneer, Bridge Builder and Statesman—A Conversation with Ambassador Edward J. Perkins," published in The Foreign Service Journal, December 2020, https://afsa.org/pioneer-bridge-builder-and-statesman-conversation-ambassador-edward-j-perkins. Republished with permission.

Ambassador Ruth A. Davis discusses the empowerment of women and education of girls in Benin with First Lady Hillary Rodham Clinton on July 13, 1995. Source: Photo courtesy of the White House, from "A Foreign Service Trailblazer—Ambassador Ruth A. Davis," published in The Foreign Service Journal, September 2016, https://afsa.org/foreign-service-trailblazer-ambassador-ruth-davis.

Social media flyer from 2021 Black History Month conversation moderated by the author and including three Black Ambassadors as speakers. The event was co-hosted by the Association of Black American Ambassadors (ABAA) and Black Professional in Intenrational Affairs (BPIA). Source: Author

Assistant Secretary of State for African Affairs (and former U.S. Ambassador to South Africa), Dr. Jendayi Frazer (center) participates with other leaders, in the U.S.-Africa Leaders Summit on December 13, 2022. Source: Courtesy of the U.S. Department of State, from the Talking Points section of The Foreign Service Journal, March 2023.

Ambassador Adrienne O'Neal visiting with the Mayor of Brava Island in Cape Verde, the African nation from which many Black Americans of African descent can trace their roots. Source: Amb O'Neal

Ambassador Mattie Sharpless being received by the President of the Central African Republic (CAR), Ange'-Felix Patasse', Bangui, CAR in November 2001. Source: Amb Sharpless

Ambassador Charles Ray, after his retirement, testifying before the U.S. Congress in 2017, regarding the overthrow of Robert Mugabe in Zimbabwe. Source: Amb Ray

Top image is Ambassador Adrienne O'Neal with General David Petraeus and Cape Verde Defense Minister at Conference on Defense in Praia in 2012.

Bottom image is Ambassador Adrienne O'Neal (third for the right) again with General Patraeus and others at the same conference. Source: Amb O'Neal

Ambassador John Jones at White House with President G. W. Bush, Secretary of State Condoleezza Rice, and others. Source: Amb Jones

Ambassador John Jones at meeting in the White House with President G. W. Bush, Vice President Dick Cheney, Secretary of State Condoleezza Rice, and others. Source: Amb Jones

Ambassador John Jones visiting an ancient religious site in Lalibela, Ethiopia during an assignment with the Office of the Inspector General to the U.S. Embassy in Ethiopia. Source: Amb Jones

Ambassador Michael Battle. Source: Amb Battle

CHAPTER 8:
JULY

July 1
1926 On this day in 1926, Arthur Lewis was born in New York, New York. Lewis was a military veteran and diplomat who would serve as U.S. Ambassador to Sierra Leone from 1983 to 1986. Lewis was also a cousin to another trailblazing Black American diplomatic leader, Colin Powell, who was the first Black American Secretary of State.

July 2
2021 On this day in 2021, Ambassador Linda Thomas-Greenfield toured a mobile COVID-19 vaccine site at Commodore Barry Park in Fort Greene, Brooklyn, New York, as part of the U.S. President's "America's Back Together" campaign. The visit was intended to highlight the progress the city and the nation had made toward safely re-opening, see community vaccination efforts firsthand, and thank frontline personnel for their crucial work combating the COVID-19 pandemic throughout the City's five boroughs and beyond. Ambassador Thomas-Greenfield was a university educator and career diplomat who served as U.S. Ambassador to Liberia from 2008 to 2012 and to the United Nations from 2021 to 2024.

July 3
2014 On this day in 2014, Ambassador Brian Nichols presented his credentials to the leadership in Peru, officially beginning his tenure in-residence as leader of the U.S. Mission in this South American nation. Nichols was a career diplomat who served as U.S. Ambassador to Peru from 2014 to 2017 and then again later to Zimbabwe from 2018 to 2021. Ambassador Nichols is also one of only five Black Americans who have earned and been confirmed with the personal rank of Career Ambassador, in recognition of especially distinguished service over a sustained period.

July 4

1993 On this day in 1993, Ambassador Edward Perkins was among those whom the *LA Times* announced President Bill Clinton's intention to nominate to a new ambassadorial post. It stated that Perkins was to be nominated as U.S. Ambassador to Australia. Ambassador Perkins was a military veteran and career diplomat who had previously served as a U.S. Ambassador on three other occasions – to Liberia from 1985 to 1986, South Africa from 1986 to 1989, and the United Nations (UN) from 1992 to 1993. Now, with this nomination, and following Senate confirmation, he would hold his fourth ambassadorial post, serving as U.S. Ambassador to Australia from 1993 to 1996.

July 5

2006 On this day in 2006, Gayleatha Brown was nominated by President George W. Bush to be U.S. Ambassador to Benin. After Senate confirmation, Brown, who was a career diplomat, would take up this post and serve as U.S. Ambassador in this small West African nation until 2009.

Major Milestone Moment

July 6

On this day in 1993, **Ambassador Aurelia Brazeal** officially ended her tenure as U.S. Ambassador to the Federated States of Micronesia, where she had served since 1990. Ambassador Brazeal had been the first ever U.S. Ambassador accredited to this Island nation. She was a career diplomat who served as U.S. Ambassador on three separate occasions, including to Micronesia from 1990 to 1993, Kenya from 1993 to 1996, and Ethiopia from 2002 to 2005. Ambassador Brazeal was also the first Black female Foreign Service Officer to rise from the entry level of the Service to its senior ranks.

July 7

1986 On this day in 1986, Ambassador George Moose officially ended his tenure as U.S. Ambassador to Benin, where he had served since 1983. Moose was a career diplomat who served as U.S. Ambassador on three separate occasions, including to Benin from 1983 to 1986, to Senegal from 1988 to 1991, and as the U.S. Permanent Representative to the European Office of the United Nations (UN) in Geneva with the rank of Ambassador from 1997 to 2001.

July 8

2014 On this day in 2014, Crystal Nix-Hines was nominated by President Barack Obama to be U.S. Permanent Representative to the United Nations Educational, Scientific, and Cultural Organization (UNESCO), with the rank of Ambassador. Following Senate confirmation, she would serve in this leadership role until 2017. Nix-Hines was an attorney, screenwriter and producer, and diplomat who focused her tenure as U.S. Ambassador to UNESCO to promote the use of science, education, and cultural engagements as tools for building a more peaceful, prosperous, and secure world.

July 9

1964 On this day in 1964, Will Mercer Cook was nominated by President Lyndon B. Johnson to be U.S. Ambassador to Senegal and simultaneously to The Gambia. Following Senate confirmation, Ambassador Cook served in this leadership role until 1966. Ambassador Cook was also the first Black American to be appointed and to serve as a U.S. Ambassador on multiple occasions. Ambassador Cook served in the African nations of Niger from 1961 to 1964 (as mentioned), Senegal from 1964 to 1966 and The Gambia from 1965 to 1966.

July 10

1977 On this day in 1977, Ambassador O. Rudolph Aggrey officially ended his tenure as U.S. Ambassador to Senegal and The Gambia, where he simultaneously served since 1973. Aggrey was a career diplomat and university educator who served as, in addition to his service as U.S. Ambassador to Senegal and The Gambia from 1973 to 1977, also later served as U.S. Ambassador to Romania from 1977 to 1981.

July 11

1981 On this day in 1981, Ambassador O. Rudolph Aggrey officially ended his tenure as U.S. Ambassador to Romania, where he had served since 1977. Aggrey was a career diplomat and university educator who, prior to his time as U.S. Ambassador to Romania, had also served as U.S. Ambassador to Senegal and The Gambia simultaneously from 1973 to 1977.

July 12

1980 On this day in 1980, Ambassador William Jones officially ended his tenure as U.S. Ambassador to Haiti, where he had served since 1977. Jones was an attorney and career diplomat who would spend much of his later career promoting international service and the Foreign Service as a career option to university students while he served as Diplomat or Ambassador-in-Residence at three different universities: Hampton University, University of Virginia, and Hampden-Sydney College.

July 13

2006 On this day in 2006, Cindy Courville was nominated by President George W. Bush to be U.S. Representative to the African Union (AU), with the rank of Ambassador. After Senate confirmation, Ambassador Courville would take up this post and serve as the first ever U.S. Ambassador to the AU. Courville was an Africa scholar and expert who would serve in this capacity as U.S. Ambassador to the AU until 2008.

July 14

1992 On this day in 1992, Joseph Segars was nominated to be U.S. Ambassador to Côte d'Ivoire. Following Senate confirmation, Ambassador Segars, a career diplomat, would serve as U.S. Ambassador to Côte d'Ivoire until 1996.

July 15

2011 On this day in 2011, Ambassador Marcia Bernicat officially ended her tenure as U.S. Ambassador to Senegal and Guinea-Bissau, where she had simultaneously served since 2008. Bernicat was a career diplomat who, in addition to her time as U.S. Ambassador to Senegal and concurrently to Guinea-Bissau from 2008 to 2011, would later serve as U.S. Ambassador to Bangladesh from 2015 to 2018.

July 16

1969 On this day in 1969, Ambassador Elliot Skinner officially ended his tenure as U.S. Ambassador to Upper Volta, which would later be called Burkina Faso. Skinner was a military veteran, anthropologist, university educator, and diplomat who would serve in this role as U.S. Ambassador to Upper Volta from 1966 to 1969.

July 17

1995 On this day in 1995, Ambassador Kenton Keith officially ended his tenure as U.S. Ambassador to Qatar where he had served since 1992. Keith was a military veteran and career diplomat who was the first Black American to lead the U.S. Mission in an Arabian Peninsula nation with the full rank and title of Ambassador. He would do so in Qatar from 1992 to 1995.

July 18

1929 On this day in 1929, Leonard Spearman, Sr., was born in Tallahassee, Florida. Spearman was a university educator and leader, public servant, and diplomat who served as U.S. Ambassador to Rwanda from 1988 to 1990 and Lesotho from 1990 to 1993.

1945 On this day in 1945, Gregory Johnson was born in Ellensburg, Virginia. Johnson was a career diplomat who served as U.S. Ambassador to Swaziland from 1999 to 2001.

July 19

1972 On this day, Ambassador Samuel Westerfield, Jr., while leading the U.S. Mission in Liberia, suffered a heart attack and passed away in 1972. Westerfield was an economist, university educator, public servant, and diplomat who served as U.S. Ambassador to Liberia from 1969 to 1972. He had been among the first Black Americans who were trained as an economist, to work in the U.S. Department of State's diplomatic service, focusing his work on the economic plight of Africa and playing a key role in developing U.S. economic policies toward the region.

July 20

1978 On this day in 1978, Ambassador Terence D. Todman presented his credentials to the leadership of Spain, officially beginning his tenure in-residence as leader of the U.S. Mission to this European nation. Ambassador Todman would serve in Spain until 1983. Ambassador Todman was the Black American who served as U.S. Ambassador on the most occasions (six times), and in 1989 he became the first Black American to be promoted to the rank of Career Ambassador. As U.S. Ambassador he served in six different countries, including: to Chad from 1969 to 1972; Guinea from 1982 to 1975. and Costa Rica from 1975 to 1977. As previously mentioned, he also served Spain from 1978 to 1983; Denmark from 1983 to 1989; and Argentina from 1989 1993.

July 21

1977 On this day in 1977, Richard Fox presented his credentials to the leadership in Trinidad and Tobago, officially beginning his tenure as U.S. Ambassador to that nation. Fox was a military veteran and career diplomat who served as U.S. Ambassador to Trinidad and Tobago from 1977 to 1979. During his career as a diplomat, one of Fox's key roles included traveling around the U.S., speaking, and encouraging more Black Americans to join the U.S. Foreign Service.

July 22

2014 On this day in 2014, Michael Lawson was nominated to be U.S. Representative to the International Civil Aviation Organization (ICAO), with the rank of Ambassador. Following Senate confirmation, Lawson, an attorney, aviation expert, and diplomat, would serve as U.S. Ambassador to the Montreal, Canada-based ICAO until 2017.

July 23

2014 On this day in 2014, Ambassador Eunice Reddick was nominated for her second ambassadorial posting, this time to be U.S. Ambassador to Niger. After Senate confirmation, Ambassador Reddick took up her post and served in this leadership position until 2017. Reddick was a career diplomat who, prior to serving as U.S. Ambassador to Niger, had previously served as U.S. Ambassador to Gabon and concurrently to São Tomé and Principe from 2007 to 2010.

July 24

1926 On this day in 1926, O. Rudolph Aggrey was born in Salisbury, North Carolina. Aggrey was a career diplomat and university educator who would serve as U.S. Ambassador to Senegal and The Gambia from 1973 to 1977, and to Romania from 1977 to 1981.

1930 On this day in 1930, Walter Carrington was born in New York, New York. Carrington was a military veteran, attorney, scholar, and diplomat who served as U.S. Ambassador to Senegal from 1980 to 1981, and to Nigeria from 1993 to 1997.

July 25
2017 On this day in 2017, Ambassador Robin Sanders' book "The Rise of Africa's Small and Medium-Sized Enterprises" was highlighted in a YouTube video and on other social media channels. Ambassador Sanders was a career diplomat who served as U.S. Ambassador to Congo from 2002 to 2005 and to Nigeria from 2007 to 2010.

July 26
1977 On this day in 1997, William Jones was announced as President Jimmy Carter's choice as U.S. Ambassador to Haiti. Jones was an attorney and career diplomat who, after Senate confirmation, served as U.S. Ambassador to Haiti from 1977 to 1980.

July 27
2020 On this day in 2020, Ambassador Marguerita Ragsdale was featured on the website of the Virginia Interscholastic Association (VIA). The article provided her bio and also discussed her induction into VIA's Hall of Fame in 2018. Ragsdale was a career diplomat who had served as U.S. Ambassador to Djibouti from 2004 to 2006.

July 28
2009 On this day in 2009, Mary Jo Wills was announced by President Barack Obama as his intended nominee to be the U.S. Ambassador to Mauritius and Seychelles. Wills was a career diplomat, and after Senate confirmation, she would go on to serve as U.S. Ambassador to Mauritius and concurrently to Seychelles from 2010 to 2011.

July 29

2013 On this day in 2013, Ambassador Larry Palmer was reported by the *Dominica News Online*, to have visited the Island nation of Dominica. Ambassador Palmer's visit was to help celebrate the four-year anniversary of the signing of a Memorandum of Understanding (MOU) between the U.S. and Dominica's Education Ministry, which had launched the American Corners at a local public library. Ambassador Palmer was a university educator and career diplomat who served as U.S. Ambassador to Honduras from 2002 to 2005, and then later to Barbados, East Caribbean, and the Organization of Eastern Caribbean States from 2012 to 2016.

Major Milestone Moment

July 30

On this day in 2015, **Ambassador Wanda Nesbitt**—then serving as Senior Vice President of the National Defense University (NDU)—participated in NDU's graduation ceremony for its Caribbean Defense and Security Course. She appeared in a NDU-published article titled "President of Guyana David Granger Speaks at Perry Center CDSC Graduation Ceremony," which highlighted the President's return as an alumnus of the program. Ambassador Nesbitt was a career diplomat who represented the U.S. as Ambassador to three nations: Madagascar from 2001 to 2004, Côte d'Ivoire from 2007 to 2010, and Namibia, from 2010 to 2013. In her role as NDU's Senior Vice President—and later, briefly as its Interim President—she championed efforts to strengthen understanding and collaboration between the U.S. military and the U.S. Department of State, emphasizing the vital, complementary roles both institutions play in advancing America's global engagement.

July 31

1936 On this day in 1936, John Burroughs was born in Washington, DC. Burroughs was an athlete, public servant, equal rights advocate, and diplomat who served as U.S. Ambassador to Malawi from 1981 to 1984 and to Uganda from 1988 to 1991.

CHAPTER 9:
AUGUST

Major Milestone Moment

August 1

On this day in 2017, **Ambassador Pamela Spratlen** met with Deputy Chairman of the Uzbekistan State Customs Committee (SCC), Bakhtiyor Raimov, in Tashkent to discuss bilateral cooperation for preventing the illicit trafficking of nuclear and other radioactive materials. During the meeting, a MOU was also signed to facilitate the U.S. Department of Energy, National Nuclear Security Administration's (DOE/NNSA's) cooperation with the Uzbek SCC, focused on long-term operations and sustainment of radiation detection systems. Spratlen was a career diplomat, who at the time was serving as U.S. Ambassador to Uzbekistan, where she would lead U.S. diplomatic efforts between 2015 and 2018. She had also previously served as U.S. Ambassador to the Kyrgyz Republic from 2011 to 2014.

August 2

2012 On this day in 2012, Ambassador Pamela Bridgewater was reported by the news outlet *Jamaicans.com* to be among the American Presidential delegation that would represent President Barack Obama in Kingston, Jamaica on August 6 to celebrate that nation's 50th Independence Anniversary. Ambassador Bridgewater was serving as U.S. Ambassador to Jamaica at the time, and the full delegation would be headed by former Secretary of State Collin Powell. Ambassador Bridgewater was a university educator and career diplomat who served as a U.S. Ambassador to three nations including to Benin from 2000 to 2002, to Ghana from 2005 to 2008, and to Jamaica from 2010 to 2013.

August 3

1990 On this day in 1990, Arlene Render was announced as President George H. W. Bush's intended nominee to be U.S. Ambassador to the Republic of The Gambia, succeeding outgoing Ambassador Ruth Washington. Following Senate confirmation, Ambassador Render would take up the first of three ambassadorships in her career, in this instance, leading the U.S. Mission in The Gambia from 1990 to 1993. She would later also serve as U.S. Ambassador to Zambia from 1996 to 1999 and to Côte d'Ivoire from 2001 to 2004.

August 4

2022 On this day in 2022, Yohannes Abraham was confirmed by the U.S. Senate to be the Representative of the United States of America to the Association of Southeast Asian Nations (ASEAN), with the rank and status of Ambassador Extraordinary and Plenipotentiary. Abraham was a career public servant who, following Senate confirmation in 2022, would serve as U.S. Ambassador to ASEAN until 2024.

August 5
1996 On this day in 1996, Ambassador Leslie Alexander presented his credentials to the leadership in Ecuador, officially beginning his tenure in-residence as leader of the U.S. Mission in this South American nation. Alexander was a career diplomat who served as U.S. Ambassador to Mauritius and the Comoros from 1993 to 1996, and then later in this post as U.S. Ambassador to Ecuador from 1996 to 1999.

August 6
2020 On this day in 2020, Natalie Brown was confirmed by the U.S. Senate as U.S. Ambassador to Uganda. Brown was a career diplomat who would serve as U.S. Ambassador to Uganda from 2020 to 2023.

August 7
1917 On this day in 1917, Melvin Evans was born in St. Croix, Virgin Islands. Evans was a medical doctor, public servant, and diplomat who would serve as U.S. Ambassador to Trinidad and Tobago from 1981 to 1984.

August 8
1993 On this day in 1993, Ambassador Arlene Render officially ended her tenure as U.S. Ambassador to The Gambia, where she had served since 1990. Ambassador Render would go on to have two other ambassadorships, serving as U.S. Ambassador to Zambia from 1996 to 1999 and then to Côte d'Ivoire from 2001 to 2004.

August 9
1993 On this date in 1993, Ambassador Aurelia Brazeal was nominated by President George H. W. Bush to be U.S. Ambassador to Kenya. Following Senate confirmation, she officially began her tenure in-residence as leader of the U.S. Mission in this African nation. Brazeal was a career diplomat who served as U.S. Ambassador on three separate

occasions, including to Micronesia from 1990 to 1993, to Kenya from 1993 to 1996, and to Ethiopia from 2002 to 2005.

August 10
2010 On this day in 2010, Ambassador Wanda Nesbitt officially ended her tenure as U.S. Ambassador to Côte d'Ivoire where she had served since 2007. Nesbit was a career diplomat who served the U.S. as Ambassador to three nations, including Madagascar from 2001 to 2004, Côte d'Ivoire from 2007 to 2010, and Namibia from 2010 to 2013.

August 11
1925 On this day in 1925, Carl Rowan was born in Ravenscroft, Tennessee. Rowan was a military veteran, journalist, and diplomat who would serve as U.S. Ambassador to Finland from 1963 to 1964. During his career, Rowan would also become the first Black American to be appointed as a Deputy Secretary of State and the first to be Director of the United States Information Agency (USIA).

August 12
2001 On this day in 2001, Ambassador William Clarke officially ended his tenure as U.S. Ambassador to Eritrea, where he had served since 1998. Clarke was a career diplomat who spent most of his diplomatic assignments working across various parts of the Department of State's Bureau of Diplomatic Security. With his appointment as U.S. Ambassador to Eritrea, he would become the first member of the Bureau of Diplomatic Security to be appointed and serve as an Ambassador.

August 13
1990 On this day in 1990, Ambassador O. Rudolph Aggrey sat down with an interviewer for the Association for Diplomatic Studies and Training's (ADST's) Oral History Project, to speak about his distinguished diplomatic career.

Aggrey was a career diplomat and university educator who served as U.S. Ambassador to Senegal and The Gambia from 1973 to 1977, and later to Romania from 1977 to 1981.

August 14

2003 On this day in 2003, Ambassador Harry Thomas, Jr. presented his credentials to the leadership of Bangladesh, officially beginning his tenure in-residence as leader of the U.S. Mission in that country. Thomas was a career diplomat who served as U.S. Ambassador to three different nations including Bangladesh from 2003 to 2005, the Philippines from 2010 to 2013, and Zimbabwe from 2016 to 2018.

August 15

1920 On this day in 1920, Samuel Adams was born in Houston, Texas. Adams was a public servant, international development expert, and diplomat who would serve as U.S. Ambassador to Niger from 1968 to 1969.

August 16

1947 On this day in 1947, Carol Moseley Braun was born in Chicago, Illinois. Moseley Braun was an attorney, public servant, U.S. Senator, and diplomat who would serve as U.S. Ambassador to New Zealand and Samoa concurrently from 1999 to 2001. Prior to this, in 1992, she had upset the incumbent Senator in the Illinois Democratic Primary and went on to become the first female Senator elected from Illinois and the first Black American woman in the U.S. Senate.

1943 On this day in 1943, Arlene Render born in Cleveland, Ohio. Render was a career diplomat who served as U.S. Ambassador on three separate occasions, including to The Gambia from 1990 to 1993, to Zambia from 1996 to 1999, and to Côte d'Ivoire from 2001 to 2004.

August 17

1921 On this day in 1921, Ruth Washington was born in Buffalo, New York. Washington was an attorney, university educator, and diplomat who was appointed as U.S. Ambassador to The Gambia in 1989. She was confirmed as U.S. Ambassador by the U.S. Senate, but tragically, she was killed in a car accident in January of 1990, in the United States, just one week prior to her departure to serve as U.S. Ambassador in The Gambia.

August 18

1975 On this day in 1975, Ambassador William Beverly Carter was the subject of a *New York Times* article entitled "Kissinger, in Tanzania Case, Affirms Curbs on Ambassadors." In the article, it was reported that the Secretary of State (Henry Kissinger), in response to negative reports of Ambassador Carter's decisions related to the release of three Stanford University students and a Dutch woman kidnapped in Tanzania, reaffirmed that "the Ambassador was a 'distinguished' emissary whose concern in the Tanzanian case was 'easily understandable.' Ambassador Carter was a journalist and career diplomat who served as U.S. Ambassador to Tanzania from 1972 to 1975, to Liberia from 1976 to 1979, and At-Large as Liaison with State & Local Government from 1979 to 1981.

August 19

1913 On this day in 1913, Hugh Smythe was born in Pittsburgh, Pennsylvania. Smythe was a military veteran, university educator, scholar, and diplomat who served as U.S. Ambassador to Syria from 1965 to 1967, making him the first ever Black American to be an Ambassador in the Middle East. He also later served as U.S. Ambassador to Malta from 1967 to 1969.

August 20

1999 On this day in 1999, Ambassador Bismarck Myrick presented his credentials to the leadership in Liberia, officially beginning his tenure in-residence as leader of the U.S. Mission in this West African nation. Myrick was a military veteran and career diplomat who served as U.S. Ambassador to Lesotho from 1995 to 1998 and Liberia from 1999 to 2002.

Major Milestone Moment

August 21

On this day in 2019, **Ambassador Marcia Bernicat** while serving as Principal Deputy Assistant Secretary of State in the Bureau of Oceans and International Environmental and Scientific Affairs, delivered remarks at the Opening Session of the Third Global Meeting of Wildlife Enforcement Networks in Geneva. In her remarks, Ambassador Bernicat outlined the U.S. stance on combatting wildlife trafficking and how it undermines economic prosperity and communities' livelihoods; encourages corruption; spreads disease; and pushes species to the brink of extinction. While doing so, she also made the connection between wildlife trafficking and U.S. national security interests. Ambassador Bernicat was a career diplomat who had previously served as U.S. Ambassador to Senegal and concurrently Guinea-Bissau from 2008 to 2011 and later to Bangladesh from 2015 to 2018. She also served as Director General of the Foreign Service and Director of Global Talent from 2022 to 2025.

August 22

2009 On this day in 2009, Ambassador Gayleatha Brown officially ended her tenure as U.S. Ambassador to Benin. Brown was a career diplomat who had served as U.S. Ambassador in this African nation since 2006.

August 23

2018 On this day in 2018 Ambassador Patrick Gaspard's opinion piece entitled "Trump's Racial Arson on South Africa: How His Tweets, Inspired by White Nationalists Lies, Will Harm an Ally" was published in the *New York Daily News.* The purpose of the article was to demonstrate how the president's Tweets about South Africa (and other countries on the continent) were ill-informed and often promoted racist and ignorant opinions about such countries. Ambassador Gaspard was a community and political organizer as well as a diplomat who served as U.S. Ambassador to South Africa from 2013 to 2016.

Major Milestone Moment

August 24

On this day in 2012, **Ambassador Charles Ray** was given a Flag Ceremony at the U.S. Department of State, in celebration of his retirement after nearly 50 years of service to the U.S. – as a member of the military and as a U.S. Foreign Service Officer. During his farewell remarks on this day, Ambassador Ray thanked many people, including two other Black American U.S. Ambassadors – **Ruth Davis** and **Aurelia Brazeal** – for the positive roles they had played in his career. Ray was a military veteran and career diplomat who served as U.S. Ambassador to Cambodia from 2002 to 2005 and then to Zimbabwe from 2009 to 2012.

August 25

1977 On this day in 1977, Ambassador Andrew Young appeared in a photograph with Tanzanian President Julius Nyerere and U.S. Vice President Walter Mondale. The image was published in *Jet* magazine as part of coverage of the official state visit of the Tanzanian President, which was the first visit to the U.S. by an African head of state during the Carter administration. Young was a minister, civil rights activist, public servant, and diplomat who served as U.S. Permanent Representative to the United Nations (UN) with the rank of Ambassador (1977-1979), the first Black American to ever hold this role and rank.

August 26

1949 On this day in 1949, Charles Stith born in St. Louis, Missouri. Stith was a minister, university educator and administrator, and diplomat who would serve as U.S. Ambassador to Tanzania from 1998 to 2001.

August 27

2010 On this day in 2010, Ambassador Robin Sanders departed from her post as leader of the U.S. Mission to Nigeria. Sanders was a career diplomat who served as U.S. Ambassador to Congo from 2002 to 2005 and then to Nigeria from 2007 to 2010.

August 28

1925 On this day in 1925, George Haley was born in Henning, Tennessee. Haley was a military veteran, attorney, public servant, and diplomat who would serve as U.S. Ambassador to The Gambia from 1998 to 2001. Haley was also the younger brother of the Pulitzer Prize winning author of *Roots*, Alex Haley.

August 29

2004 On this day in 2004, Ambassador Gina Abercrombie-Winstanley was the subject of an article published by the independent news forum serving Returned Peace Corps

Volunteers (RPCVs), called *Peace Corps Online.* Entitled "Special Report: Diplomat and Oman RPCV Gina Abercrombie-Winstanley." The article discussed Abercrombie-Winstanley, who was a former U.S. Peace Corps volunteer in Oman from 1980 to 1982, and her current (at the time) service as U.S. Consul General in Saudi Arabia. It called attention to her unlikely leadership position in the gender conservative Saudi Arabia. It also covered her journey from Cleveland, Ohio (where she was born and raised) to Jeddah, Saudi Arabia. Later in her career, Abercrombie-Winstanley was a career diplomat, who served as U.S. Ambassador to Malta from 2012 to 2016 and later as the Chief Diversity and Inclusion Officer for the Department of State from 2021 to 2023.

2024 On this day in 2024, Ambassador Arthur Brown was the subject of an article in the University of Virginia's (UVA's) online news outlet, *UVA Today*. The article, titled "One Gutsy Phone Call Took Alumnus From a Dirt Road to a United States Embassy," outlines Ambassador Brown's life from growing up on a dirt road in Keswick, Virginia (near Charlottesville) to his attendance at UVA. From there he walked on the football team to his distinguished career as a U.S. diplomat. That diplomatic career, which included service representing the United States in nine countries, also included his service as U.S. Ambassador to Ecuador, where he led the U.S. Mission from 2024 to 2025.

August 30

1998 On this day in 1998, Ambassador Shirley Barnes presented her credentials to the leadership in Madagascar, officially beginning her tenure in-residence as U.S. Ambassador to that African Island nation. Barnes was a career diplomat and her service as U.S. Ambassador to Madagascar lasted from 1998 to 2001.

2010 On this day in 2010, Ambassador Robin Sanders was the subject of the online news outlet *The Nigerian Voice* when it published a short article about her departure as U.S. Ambassador to Nigeria. In the article, the author thanks the Ambassador for "believing in this nation, for investing her time and energy in it, for standing by it during one of its trying periods..." and more.

August 31

2001 On this day in 2001, Roy Austin was announced as President George W. Bush's intended nominee to be U.S. Ambassador to Trinidad and Tobago. Following U.S. Senate confirmation, Ambassador Austin would serve in this capacity until 2009. Austin was a university educator, scholar, and diplomat.

CHAPTER 10:
SEPTEMBER

September 1

2022 On this day in 2022, Ambassador Timmy Davis was celebrated in an article by the University of Southern Mississippi, in which he had enrolled in 1988. The article was entitled "Former USM Student Climbs Ladder of Foreign Service to U.S. Ambassador. Timmy Davis was a military veteran and career diplomat who served as U.S. Ambassador to Qatar from 2022 to 2025.

2022 On this date in 2022, Ambassador-Designate Yohannes Abraham participated in a roundtable hosted by the U.S. Association of Southeast Asian Nations (ASEAN) Business Council. There, he shared his insights on the importance of strong U.S. relations with the members of the ASEAN. Abraham had recently been nominated by President Joe Biden and confirmed by the U.S. Senate as U.S. Ambassador to the ASEAN, and he was preparing for his official swearing-in. Following the swearing-in ceremony, Ambassador Yohannes would travel to Jakarta, Indonesia, where he would serve as U.S. Ambassador to the ASEAN from 2022 to 2024.

Major Milestone Moment

September 2

On this day in 1998, **Ambassador Pierre-Richard Prosper** (prior to becoming an Ambassador), while serving as the lead prosecutor for the United Nation's (UN's) International Criminal Court (ICC), saw his hard work yield groundbreaking results. This was the day the ICC handed down the first ever conviction for the defined crime of "genocide". In this landmark judgment, the Rwandan political leader Jean-Paul Akayesu was found guilty and convicted of genocide, inciting genocide, and crimes against humanity. Additionally, the conviction included the first time an international court punished sexual violence in a civil war and the first time rape was successfully prosecuted as an act of genocide, intended to destroy a group. Prosper would later become U.S. Ambassador-At-Large for War Crimes Issues after appointment as such by President George W. Bush, and confirmation by the U.S. Senate. He served as U.S. Ambassador-At-Large from 2001 to 2005.

September 3

2015 On this day in 2015, Ambassador Cynthia Akuetteh was reported in a Press Release by the U.S. Customs and Border Protection (CBP) to be among the senior U.S. officials present at the signing of a new security and trade agreement between the U.S. and Gabon. The Release stated that the U.S. signed a Customs Mutual Assistance Agreement (CMAA) with Gabon on August 27, and it marked a significant milestone in collaboration on security and trade facilitation between the two countries. U.S. Ambassador to Gabon, Cynthia Akuetteh, was among the senior officials leading the signing of the Agreement, along with several other key officials from the two nations. Ambassador Akuetteh, who had played a key role in negotiating the Agreement, was a career diplomat who served as U.S. Ambassador to Gabon and concurrently to São Tomé and Príncipe from 2014 to 2018.

September 4

1964 On this day in 1964, Ambassador Clifton Wharton, Sr., ended his tenure as U.S. Ambassador to Norway, where he had served since April 16, 1961. Wharton was an attorney and career diplomat whose service as U.S. Ambassador to Norway, made him the first Black American to serve as a U.S. Ambassador in a European country.

September 5

2022 On this day in 2022, Ambassador Timmy Davis was reported by the *Gulf Times* online news to have arrived in Qatar. Davis was appointed by President Jo Biden to be U.S. Ambassador to Qatar back in March 2022 and, following Senate confirmation, was arriving to assume his leadership of the U.S. Mission in this small but important Middle East nation. He would do so through 2025.

Major Milestone Moment

September 6

On this day in 2018, **Dereck Hogan** was confirmed by the U.S. Senate as U.S. Ambassador to Moldova. Ambassador Hogan had begun his journey into the U.S. Foreign Service, as a Thomas R. Pickering Foreign Affairs Graduate Fellow in 1993. Upon completing his Pickering Fellowship, he entered the U.S. Foreign Service and ultimately, was appointed as U.S. Ambassador to Moldova by the President in 2018. This would make him the first ever Pickering Fellow alum to be appointed and confirmed as a U.S. Ambassador. He would go on to lead U.S. efforts in Moldova from 2018 to 2021.

September 7
1973 On this day in 1973, Reuben Brigety was born in Jacksonville, Florida. Brigety was a military veteran, university educator, international humanitarian expert, and diplomat. He served as U.S. Representative to the African Union (AU) with the rank of Ambassador from 2013 to 2015, and as U.S. Ambassador to South Africa, beginning in 2022, where he led until 2025.

September 8
2006 On this day in 2006, Ambassador Gayleatha Brown presented her credentials to the leadership in Benin, officially beginning her tenure as U.S. Ambassador to this African nation. She would serve in this leadership role until 2009.

September 9
1928 On this day in 1928, Maurice Bean was born in Gary, Indiana. Bean was a career diplomat who would serve as U.S. Ambassador to the East Asian and Pacific Island nation of Burma (now called Myanmar) from 1977 to 1979. This made him the first Black American to serve as a U.S. Ambassador in this region of the world.

September 10
2018 On this day in 2018, Ambassador Reuben Brigety, while serving as Dean of the George Washington University Elliott School of International Affairs, spoke on the Young Professional of Washington, DC's podcast "Matters of State" about his experience representing the U.S. within the African Union (AU). In the interview, he was optimistic about the economic development prospects of the AU and the key role it played in interstate relations across the continent. Prior to his time as Dean of the Elliott School, Brigety had served as U.S. Ambassador to the AU from 2013 to 2015. He would also later serve as U.S. Ambassador to South Africa from 2022 to 2025.

September 11

1980 On this day in 1980, Ambassador Barbara Watson ended her tenure as Assistant Secretary of State for Consular Affairs. Watson was the first woman and first Black American to ever serve as an Assistant Secretary of State. She would later be appointed and serve as U.S. Ambassador to Malaysia from 1980 to 1981.

September 12

2014 On this day in 2014, Ambassador Eunice Reddick presented her credentials to the leadership in Niger, officially beginning her tenure in-residence as leader of the U.S. Mission to this African nation. Reddick was a career diplomat who served as U.S. Ambassador to Gabon and concurrently to São Tomé and Principe from 2007 to 2010, and then again to Niger from 2014 to 2017.

September 13

2013 On this day in 2013, Ambassador Bisa Williams officially ended her tenure as U.S. Ambassador to the African nation of Niger. Williams was a career diplomat who had served as U.S. Ambassador to Niger since 2010.

Major Milestone Moment

September 14

On this day in 2010, as the United Nations (UN) 65th General Assembly opened, the top U.S. diplomats in the UN system were Black American women. This included the U.S. Representative to the UN, with the rank of **Ambassador, Susan Rice** leading the U.S. Mission to the UN in New York from 2009 to 2013; **Ambassador Ertharin Cousin** who served as U.S. Representative to the UN Agencies for Food and Agriculture in Rome from 2010 to 2012; and **Ambassador Betty King** who served as U.S. Representatives to the European Office of the UN in Geneva from 2010 to 2013.

September 15

2021 On this day in 2021, Ambassador Marcia Bernicat testified before the U.S. Senate Foreign Relations Committee regarding her nomination to be Director General of the Foreign Service and Director of Global Talent Management. Bernicat was a career diplomat who served as U.S. Ambassador to Senegal and concurrently Guinea-Bissau from 2008 to 2011 and to Bangladesh from 2015 to 2018.

September 16

1976 On this day in 1976, Charles James was nominated by President Gerald Ford to be U.S. Ambassador to the African nation of Niger. Following a successful confirmation by the U.S. Senate, Ambassador James would lead the U.S. Mission in this nation from 1976 to 1979. James was a military veteran, attorney, public servant, and diplomat.

September 17

2013 On this day in 2013, Ambassador Tulinabo Mushingi presented his credentials to the leadership of Burkina Faso, officially beginning his tenure in residence as the leader of the U.S. Mission in this African nation. Mushingi was a career diplomat who served as U.S. Ambassador to Burkina Faso from 2013 to 2016, and after that, to Senegal and concurrently Guinea-Bissau from 2017 to 2021, and to Angola and São Tomé and Principe from 2021 to 2024.

September 18

2014 On this day in 2014, the U.S. Mission to the International Organizations in Geneva posted on its website the official Biography of Ambassador Robert Wood, U.S. Permanent Representative to the Conference on Disarmament and U.S. Special Representative for Biological and Toxin Weapons Convention (BCW), informing the public of the credentials of the new U.S. Ambassador to this important global body. Wood was a career diplomat who served as Ambassador to this body from 2014 to 2020. He would later also be appointed and serve as Alternate Representative of the U.S. for Special Political Affairs in the United Nations, with the rank of Ambassador, from 2022 to 2025.

September 19
2013 On this day in 2013, Reuben Brigety was nominated by President Barack Obama to be the United States Representative to the African Union (AU), with the rank of Ambassador. After Senate confirmation, Ambassador Brigety would serve at the AU in Addis Ababa, Ethiopia, until 2015. Brigety was a military veteran, university educator, international humanitarian expert, and diplomat who, in addition to his service as U.S. Ambassador to the AU, served as U.S. Ambassador to South Africa from 2022 to 2025.

September 20
2012 On this day in 2012, Ambassador Makila James presented her credentials to the leadership of Swaziland (now called Eswatini), officially beginning her tenure in-residence as the leader of the U.S. Mission in this southern African nation. James was a career diplomat who would serve as U.S. Ambassador to Swaziland until 2015.

September 21
2007 On this day in 2007, Ambassador Maurice Parker presented his credentials to the leadership of Swaziland (now called Eswatini), officially beginning his tenure in-residence as the leader of the U.S. Mission to this Southern African nation. Parker was a career diplomat who served as U.S. Ambassador to Swaziland until 2009.

September 22
1952 On this day in 1952, Daniel W. Yohannes was born in Addis Ababa, Ethiopia. Yohannes was a banking and investment expert and diplomat who would serve as U.S. Representative to the Organization for Economic

Cooperation and Development (OECD) in Paris, with the rank of Ambassador from 2014 to 2017.

2013 On this day in 2013, Ambassador Michael Battle officially ended his tenure as the Representative of the U.S.A. to the African Union (AU), with the rank of Ambassador, where he had served since 2009. Battle was a religious leader, military veteran, university educator, and diplomat who served as U.S. Ambassador to the AU from 2009 to 2013, and later as U.S. Ambassador to Tanzania from 2023 to 2025.

Major Milestone Moment

September 23

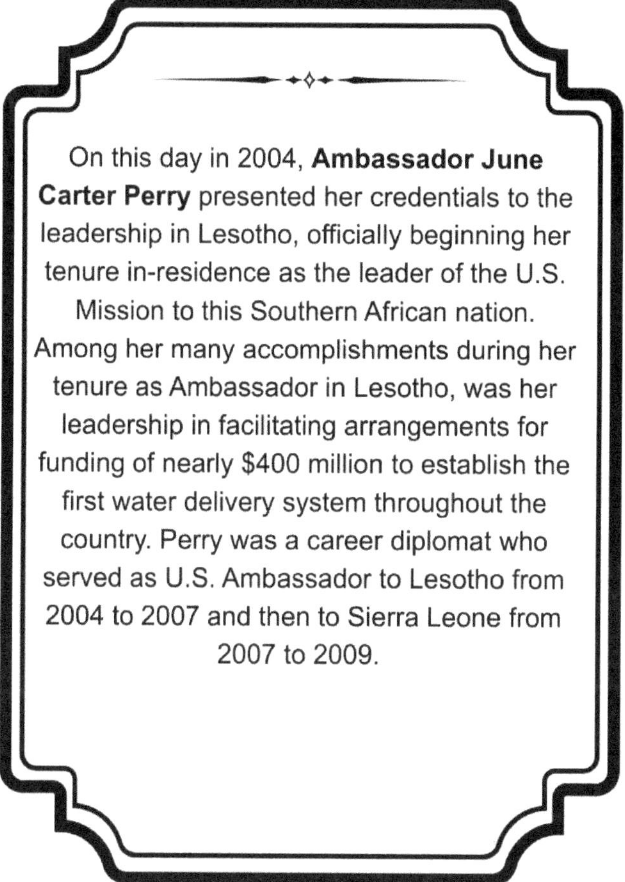

On this day in 2004, **Ambassador June Carter Perry** presented her credentials to the leadership in Lesotho, officially beginning her tenure in-residence as the leader of the U.S. Mission to this Southern African nation. Among her many accomplishments during her tenure as Ambassador in Lesotho, was her leadership in facilitating arrangements for funding of nearly $400 million to establish the first water delivery system throughout the country. Perry was a career diplomat who served as U.S. Ambassador to Lesotho from 2004 to 2007 and then to Sierra Leone from 2007 to 2009.

September 24

2013 On this day in 2013, Dwight Bush testified before the U.S. Senate Foreign Relations Committee as part of his confirmation hearing to be U.S. Ambassador to Morocco. Following successful Senate confirmation, Ambassador Bush would serve as U.S. Ambassador to this northern African nation from 2014 to 2017. Prior to this, Ambassador Bush had a successful career as a finance, banking, and corporate manager.

September 25

1949 On this day in 1949, John Hicks, Sr. was born in Goldsboro, North Carolina. Hicks was an international development expert, university administrator, and career diplomat who served as U.S. Ambassador to Eritrea from 1996 to 1997.

September 26

2014 On this day in 2014, *The Washington Post* published a brief online tribute and obituary of Ambassador John Burroughs, who had passed away on Thursday, September 11, of that year. Burroughs was an athlete, public servant, equal rights advocate, and diplomat who served as U.S. Ambassador to Malawi from 1981 to 1984 and then to Uganda from 1988 to 1991.

September 27

2005 On this day in 2005, Ambassador Roger Pierce presented his credentials to the leadership of Cape Verde, officially beginning his tenure in-residence as the leader of the U.S. Mission to this African nation. Pierce, a career diplomat, would serve as U.S. Ambassador to Cape Verde until 2007.

September 28

2021 On this day in 2021, Ambassador Todd Robinson was confirmed by the U.S. Senate to be Assistant Secretary of State in the Bureau of International Narcotics and Law

Enforcement Affairs. Robinson, a journalist and career diplomat, had previously served as U.S. Ambassador to Guatemala from 2014 to 2017.

September 29

1951 On this day in 1951, J. Steven Rhodes was born in New Orleans, Louisiana. Rhodes was an athlete, public servant, businessman, and diplomat who would briefly serve as U.S. Ambassador to Zimbabwe in 1990.

September 30

2010 On this day in 2010, Ambassador Helen Reed-Rowe presented her credentials to the leadership of Palau, officially beginning her tenure in-residence as the leader of the U.S. Mission in this East Asia and Pacific Island nation. Reed-Rowe, a career diplomat, would serve as U.S. Ambassador in Palau until 2013.

CHAPTER 11:
OCTOBER

October 1
1977 On this day in 1977, Ambassador Mabel Murphy Smythe presented her credentials to the President of Cameroon, officially beginning her tenure, in-residence as leader of the U.S. Mission in Equatorial Guinea. Murphy-Smythe was a university educator, public servant, and diplomat. Her appointment to Cameroon made her the first Black American female to serve as U.S. Ambassador to an African nation. She would hold this position until 1980, and during the latter part of this term, Ambassador Smythe was also be appointed to serve concurrently as U.S. Ambassador to the small African nation of Equatorial Guinea, which she did from 1979 to 1980.

October 2
1936 On this day in 1936, Jerome Cooper was born in Lafayette, Louisiana. Cooper was a military veteran, public servant, business leader, and diplomat who would serve as U.S. Ambassador to Jamaica from 1994 to 1997.

October 3
1969 On this day in 1969, Ambassador Samuel Adams officially ended his tenure as U.S. Ambassador to the Sub-Saharan African Nation of Niger. Adams was a public servant, international development expert, and diplomat who served as U.S. Ambassador to Niger from 1968 to 1969.

Major Milestone Moment

October 4

On this day in 2011, the *Cleveland Jewish News* posted an updated version of its article "Cleveland Hts. Native Takes Road Less Traveled" which focused on the career trajectory of Cleveland-born, **Gina Abercrombie-Winstanley**. She was a career diplomat who served as U.S. Ambassador to Malta from 2012 to 2016. Prior to that appointment, Ambassador Abercrombie-Winstanley had also been the first American woman to lead a U.S. consulate, as Counsel General, in the gender-conservative Kingdom of Saudi Arabia (2004). She would later serve as the Department of State's Chief Diversity and Inclusion Officer from 2021 to 2023.

October 5

1994 On this day in 1994, President Bill Clinton nominated Jerome Cooper to be U.S. Ambassador to Jamaica. Cooper was a military veteran, public servant, business leader, and diplomat. Following this presidential nomination and successful Senate confirmation, he served as U.S. Ambassador to Jamaica from 1994 to 1997.

October 6

2008 On this day in 2008, President George W. Bush appointed C. Steven McGann to be U.S. Ambassador to five Pacific Island nations, including Fiji, Kiribati, Nauru, Tonga, and Tuvalu. McGann was a career diplomat, and following his presidential appointment and successful Senate confirmation, he would serve as U.S. Ambassador to these five nations from 2009 to 2011.

Major Milestone Moment

October 7

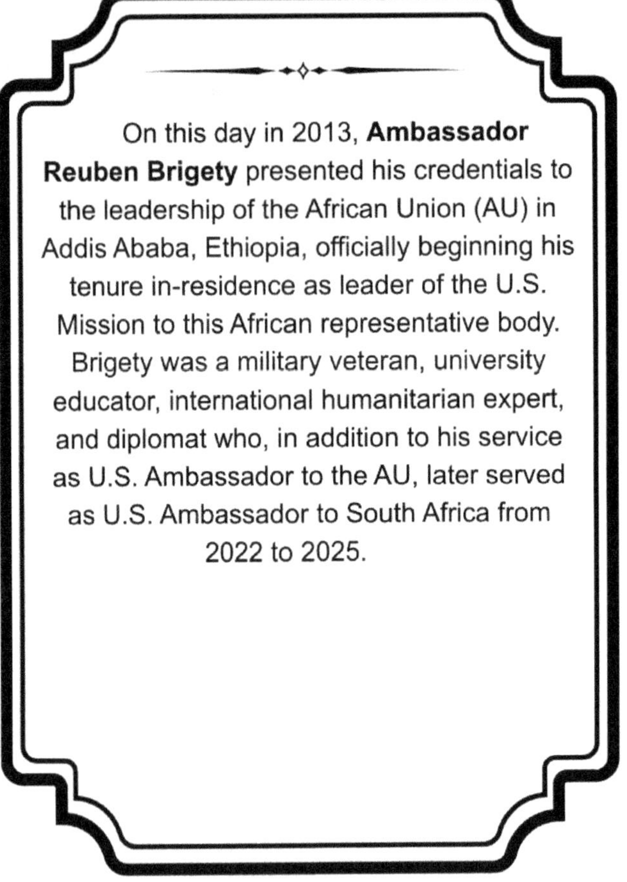

On this day in 2013, **Ambassador Reuben Brigety** presented his credentials to the leadership of the African Union (AU) in Addis Ababa, Ethiopia, officially beginning his tenure in-residence as leader of the U.S. Mission to this African representative body. Brigety was a military veteran, university educator, international humanitarian expert, and diplomat who, in addition to his service as U.S. Ambassador to the AU, later served as U.S. Ambassador to South Africa from 2022 to 2025.

October 8

2015 On this day in 2015, Carolyn P. Alsup was confirmed by the Senate as U.S. Ambassador to The Gambia. Alsup was a career diplomat who would serve as U.S. Ambassador to The Gambia from 2015 to 2016.

October 9

1997 On this day in 1997, President Bill Clinton nominated Betty King to be Alternate U.S. Representative to the United Nations (UN) General Assembly and U.S. Representative to the UN Economic and Social Council (ECOSOC), with the rank of Ambassador. King was a university educator, public servant, philanthropist, and diplomat. Following her presidential nomination and successful Senate confirmation, she would serve in these dual roles at the UN from 1997 to 2001. She would also later serve as U.S. Representative to the European Office of the UN in Geneva from 2010 to 2013 all with the rank of Ambassador.

October 10

1991 On this day in 1991, Ambassador Charles Baquet presented his credentials to the leadership of Djibouti, officially beginning his tenure in-residence as the leader of the U.S. Mission to this Sub-Saharan African nation. Baquet was a career diplomat who would serve as U.S. Ambassador to Djibouti from 1991 to 1993.

October 11

2005 On this day in 2005, Ambassador Pamela Bridgewater presented her credentials to the leadership in Ghana, officially beginning her tenure in-residence as the leader of the U.S. Mission to this Sub-Saharan African nation. Bridgewater was a university educator and career diplomat who served as a U.S. Ambassador to three nations including: Benin from 2000 to 2002, Ghana from 2005 to 2008, and Jamaica from 2010 to 2013.

October 12

1979 On this day in 1979, President Jimmy Carter nominated Horace Dawson to be U.S. Ambassador to Botswana. Dawson was a military veteran, career diplomat, and university educator. Following his presidential nomination and successful Senate confirmation, he would serve as U.S. Ambassador to Botswana from 1979 to 1982.

October 13

1936 On this day in 1936, Donald McHenry was born in St. Louis, Missouri. McHenry was a scholar, corporate governor, university educator, and diplomat who would serve as U.S. Permanent Representative to the United Nations (UN) with the rank of Ambassador from 1979 to 1981. He would also later join the Board of the Coca-Cola Company (1981), making him the first Black American Board Member of this major global corporation.

October 14

1980 On this day in 1980, Ambassador Clinton Knox passed away. Knox was a military veteran, university educator, and career diplomat who served as U.S. Ambassador to the West African Republic of Dahomey (now called Benin) from 1964 to 1969, and Haiti from 1969 to 1973.

1975 On this day in 1975, Ambassador William Carter officially ended his tenure as U.S. Ambassador to Tanzania. Carter was a journalist and career diplomat who served as U.S. Ambassador to Tanzania from 1972 to 1975, to Liberia from 1976 to 1979, and At-Large as Liaison with State and Local Government from 1979 to 1981.

October 15

1998 On this day in 1998, Ambassador George Haley presented his credentials to the leadership in The Gambia, officially beginning his tenure in-residence as the leader of the U.S. Mission to this Sub-Saharan African nation. Haley was a military veteran, attorney, public servant, and diplomat who served as U.S. Ambassador to The Gambia from 1998 to 2001. Notably, and on a personal level, Ambassador Haley was also the younger brother of Alex Haley, the Pulitzer Prize-winning author of *Roots*.

October 16

1980 On this day in 1980, Ambassador Walter Carrington presented his credentials to the leadership in Senegal, officially beginning his tenure in-residence as the leader of the U.S. Mission in this Sub-Saharan African nation. Carrington was a military veteran, attorney, scholar, and diplomat who served as U.S. Ambassador to Senegal from 1980 to 1981, and then to Nigeria from 1993 to 1997.

October 17

1925 On this day in 1925, Theodore Britton, Jr. was born in North Augusta, South Carolina. Britton was a military veteran, public servant, and diplomat who would serve as U.S. Ambassador to Barbados and Grenada from 1974 to 1977.

October 18

2001 On this day in 2001, Ambassador Gregory Johnson officially ended his tenure as U.S. Ambassador to Swaziland. Johnson was a career diplomat who served as U.S. Ambassador to Swaziland from 1999 to 2001.

October 19

2011 On this day in 2011, President Barack Obama nominated Adrienne O'Neal to be U.S. Ambassador to the Sub-Saharan African nation of Cape Verde. O'Neal was a career diplomat, and following her presidential nomination and Senate confirmation, she served as U.S. Ambassador to Cape Verde until 2015.

October 20

2013 On this day in 2013, Ambassador Suzan Johnson Cook officially ended her tenure as Ambassador-at-Large for

International Religious Freedom. Cook was a religious leader, motivational speaker, and diplomat who served as U.S. Ambassador-at-Large for International Religious Freedom from 2011 to 2013.

October 21
1977 On this day in 1977, President Richard Nixon nominated O. Rudolph Aggrey to be U.S. Ambassador to the European nation of Romania. Following Senate confirmation, Ambassador Aggrey would serve in this role until 1981. Previously, he had also served as U.S. Ambassador to The Gambia from 1973 to 1977.

October 22
1917 On this day in 1917, Franklin Williams was born in New York (Queens), New York. Williams was a military veteran, civil rights attorney, and diplomat who would serve as U.S. Ambassador to Ghana from 1965 to 1968.

1925 On this day in 1925, Richard Fox, Jr., was born in Cincinnati, Ohio. Fox was a military veteran and career diplomat who would serve as U.S. Ambassador to Trinidad and Tobago from 1977 to 1979.

1948 On this day in 1948, Francis Taylor was born in Washington, DC. Taylor was a military leader, intelligence and security expert, and diplomat who would serve as Coordinator of Counterterrorism and Director, Office to Monitor and Combat Trafficking in Persons with the rank of Ambassador, from 2001 to 2004; and, then later as Assistant Secretary, Bureau of Diplomatic Security & Director, Office of Foreign Missions also with the rank of Ambassador, from 2002 to 2005.

October 23
2016 On this day in 2016, Ambassador Pierre-Richard Prosper was featured in the *The New York Daily News* published article entitled, "Documentary on Akayesu Case

Makes World Premiere at UN; Reviewers Call It 'Riveting', 'Courtroom Thriller." The documentary was about the prosecution of rape as a war crime, with a central figure in that case being future Ambassador Pierre-Richard Prosper, who at the time, was one of two attorneys for the United Nations' International Criminal Tribunal responsible for trying the 1994 Rwandan genocide perpetrators including Jean-Paul Akayesu. During that process, Prosper and his fellow prosecutor were responsible for getting sexual violence, particularly rape, classified as a war crime for the first time in history. Prosper was later appointed by President George W. Bush as Ambassador-at-Large for War Crimes, where he served from 2001 to 2005.

October 24

1996 On this day in 1996, Ambassador Sharon Wilkinson presented her credentials to the leadership in Burkina Faso, officially beginning her tenure in-residence as leader of the U.S. Mission in this African nation. Wilkinson was a career diplomat who served as U.S. Ambassador to Burkina Faso from 1996 to 1999, and then again to Mozambique from 2000 to 2003.

Major Milestone Moment

October 25

On this day in 2017, **Ambassador Eunice Reddick** officially ended her tenure as U.S. Ambassador to the Sub-Saharan African nation of Niger, where she had served since 2014. She had also previously served as U.S. Ambassador to Gabon and concurrently São Tomé and Principe from 2007 to 2010. During her career, Ambassador Reddick also used her leadership platform to promote diplomatic careers among Black students, which she did during a 2010 assignment as Diplomat-in-Residence at Howard University, and she continues to do as a member of the Executive Committee of the Association of Black American Ambassadors (ABAA) as of the time of writing (2025).

October 26

1998 On this day in 1998, President Bill Clinton nominated George Staples to be U.S. Ambassador to the Sub-Saharan African nation of Rwanda. Following Senate confirmation, Ambassador Staples would serve in this role until 2001. He would also later serve as U.S. Ambassador to Cameroon and concurrently to Equatorial Guinea from 2001 to 2004.

October 27

2010 On this day in 2010, Ambassador Harry Thomas, Jr., presented his credentials to the leadership in the Philippines, officially beginning his tenure in-residence as U.S. Ambassador to this Southeast Asian Island nation. Ambassador Thomas would serve in this role until 2013. Also, he had previously served as U.S. Ambassador to Bangladesh from 2003 to 2005 and later serve as U.S. Ambassador to Zimbabwe from 2016 to 2018.

2004 On this day in 2004, Ambassador Joyce Barr presented her credentials to the leadership in Namibia, officially beginning her tenure in-residence, as U.S. Ambassador to this Sub-Saharan African nation. Barr, a career diplomat, would serve in this role as U.S. Ambassador until 2007.

October 28

1976 On this day in 1976, Ambassador Ronald Palmer presented his credentials to the leadership in Togo, officially beginning his tenure in-residence, as U.S. Ambassador to this Sub-Saharan African nation. Ambassador Palmer served in this role until 1978. He also later served as U.S. Ambassador to Malaysia from 1981 to 1983 and U.S. Ambassador to Mauritius from 1986 to 1989.

October 29

2007 On this day in 2007, Ambassador Robin Sanders was nominated by President George W. Bush to be U.S. Ambassador to Nigeria. After her Senate Confirmation, she would officially become the first Black American female to serve as U.S. Ambassador to this, Africa's most populous nation where she would serve until 2010. Ambassador Sanders had also previously served as U.S. Ambassador to Congo from 2002 to 2005.

October 30

1983 On this day in 1983, Ambassador Ronald Palmer officially ended his tenure as U.S. Ambassador to Malaysia, where he had served since 1981. He had also previously served as U.S. Ambassador to Togo from 1976 to 1978 and later served as U.S. Ambassador to Mauritius from 1986 to 1989.

Major Milestone Moment

October 31

On this day in 2020, African News 24 quoted **Dr. John Nkengasong** of the Africa Centres for Disease Control and Prevention (Africa CDC), as warning the continent that it must "...prepare for the second wave..." of the COVID-19 virus. The article was entitled "AFRICACOVID-19: Africa CDC Warns SA, Nigeria, Others of Second Wave." Dr. Nkengasong at that time was serving as the Founding Director of the Africa CDC. He would later, in 2022, be appointed by U.S. President Joe Biden as U.S. Ambassador-At-Large with the responsibility as Coordinator of U.S. Government Activities to Combat HIV/AIDS Globally and as head of the President's Emergency Plan for AIDS Relief (PEPFAR). This made him the first African-born, American to head PEPFAR, and he would serve in this role until 2025.

CHAPTER 12:
NOVEMBER

November 1

2019 On this day in 2019, the Ministry of Defense in Moldova released word of the operationalization of a renovated training facility at its National Army Training Center, which was all part of the Global Peace Operations Initiative (GPOI), supported by the U.S. government. In attendance at the event to launch these renovations was U.S. Ambassador to Moldova, Dereck Hogan, a career diplomat. Hogan served as U.S. Ambassador to Moldova from 2018 to 2021. He was on hand to reiterate the U.S. commitment to Moldova as it sought to support regional stability and security partially through joint training of soldiers from the region, and providing them with opportunities to train together for foreign missions.

Major Milestone Moment

November 2

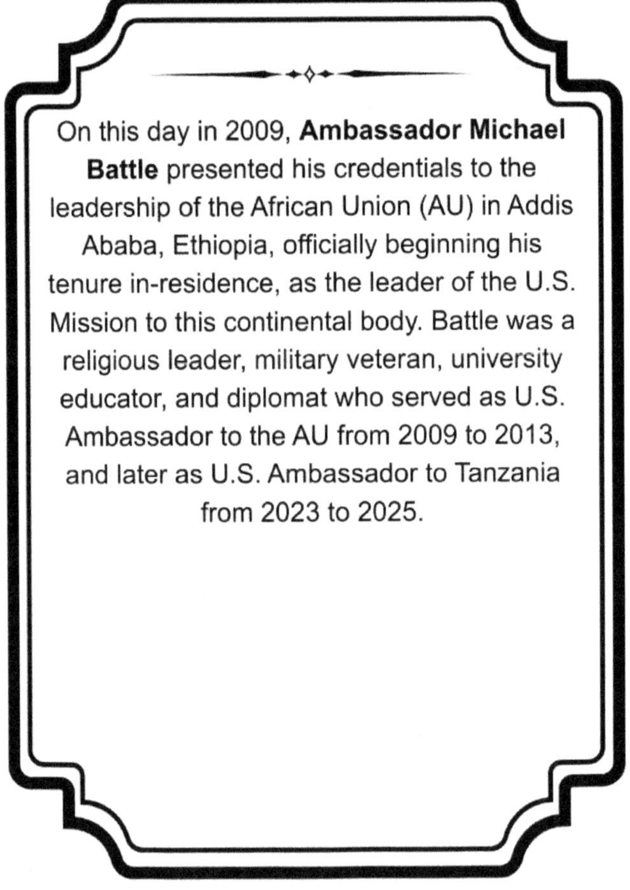

On this day in 2009, **Ambassador Michael Battle** presented his credentials to the leadership of the African Union (AU) in Addis Ababa, Ethiopia, officially beginning his tenure in-residence, as the leader of the U.S. Mission to this continental body. Battle was a religious leader, military veteran, university educator, and diplomat who served as U.S. Ambassador to the AU from 2009 to 2013, and later as U.S. Ambassador to Tanzania from 2023 to 2025.

November 3

2010 On this day in 2010, Ambassador Pamela Bridgewater presented her diplomatic credentials to the leadership in Jamaica, officially beginning her tenure in-residence as the leader of the U.S. Mission to this Caribbean Island nation. Bridgewater was a university educator and career diplomat who served as a U.S. Ambassador to three nations including to Benin from 2000 to 2002, Ghana from 2005 to 2008, and Jamaica from 2010 to 2013.

November 4

1924 On this day in 1924, Clarence Ferguson, Jr., was born in Wilmington, North Carolina. Ferguson was a military veteran, attorney, and diplomat who would serve as U.S. Ambassador to Uganda from 1970 to 1972.

November 5

2002 On this day in 2002, Ambassador Richard Baltimore presented his diplomatic credentials to the leadership in Oman, officially beginning his tenure in-residence as the leader of the U.S. Mission in this Middle Eastern nation. Baltimore was an attorney and career diplomat who served as U.S. Ambassador to Oman from 2002 to 2006.

November 6

1938 On this day in 1938, Joseph Segars was born in Hartsville, South Carolina. Segars was an educator and diplomat who served as U.S. Ambassador to Cape Verde from 1992 to 1996.

1989 On this day in 1989, Terrance Todman was appointed as a Career Ambassador. Todman had a distinguished career, beginning in the U.S. military and ending as a diplomatic leader who had the distinction of being a U.S. Ambassador more than any other Black American in history (six total), including Chad from 1969 to 1972; Guinea from 1972 to 1975; Costa Rica from 1974 to 1977; Spain from

1978 to 1983; Denmark from 1983 to 1989; and Argentina from 1989 to 1993.

November 7

1999 On this day in 1999, Ambassador James Joseph officially ended his tenure as U.S. Ambassador to South Africa, where he served since 1995. Joseph was a military veteran, minister, university educator, public servant, and diplomat who served as U.S. Ambassador to South Africa from 1995 to 1999.

November 8

1977 On this day in 1977, Ambassador Maurice Bean presented his credentials to the leadership in Burma, officially beginning his tenure in-residence as the leader of the U.S. Mission in this Southeast Asian nation. Bean was a career diplomat who served as U.S. Ambassador to this East Asian and Pacific Island nation from 1977 to 1979, making him the first Black American to serve in this role in that region of the world.

November 9

1948 On this day in 1948, Leslie Alexander was born in Frankfurt, Germany. Alexander was a career diplomat who would serve as U.S. Ambassador to Mauritius and the Comoros from 1993 to 1996, and then again to Ecuador from 1996 to 1999.

November 10

1990 On this day in 1990, Ambassador Leonard Spearman, Sr., officially ended his tenure as U.S. Ambassador to Rwanda. Spearman was a university educator and leader, public servant, and diplomat who served as U.S. Ambassador to Rwanda from 1988 to 1990, and later to Lesotho from 1990 to 1993.

November 11

1931 On this day in 1931, Wilbert LeMelle was born in New Iberia, Louisiana. LeMelle was a military veteran, university educator, international development expert, and diplomat who would serve as U.S. Ambassador to Kenya and simultaneously to the Island Nation of The Seychelles from 1977 to 1980.

2013 On this day in 2013, Ambassador Robin Sanders published a book entitled *The Legendary Uli Women of Nigeria: Their Life Stories in Signs, Symbols, and Motifs*. Sanders was a career diplomat who served as U.S. Ambassador to Congo from 2002 to 2005 and then to Nigeria from 2007 to 2010.

November 12

1933 On this day in 1933, Diane Watson was born in Los Angeles, California. Watson was an educator, public servant, U.S. Congresswoman, and diplomat who would serve as U.S. Ambassador to the Federated States of Micronesia from 1999 to 2001.

1938 On this day in 1938, Delano Lewis, Jr., was born in Arkansas City, Kansas. Lewis was an attorney, businessman, and diplomat who would serve as U.S. Ambassador to South Africa from 1999 to 2001. Just prior to that appointment, he had served as the President and CEO of National Public Radio (in 1998), making him the first Black American to hold that position.

1939 On this day in 1939, Kenton Keith was born in Kansas City, Missouri. Keith was a military veteran and career diplomat who would serve as U.S. Ambassador to Qatar from 1992 to 1995, which made him the first Black American to be U.S. Ambassador in an Arabian Peninsula country.

November 13

1969 On this day in 1969, Ambassador Clinton Knox presented his diplomatic credentials to the leadership in Haiti, officially beginning his tenure in-residence as the leader of the U.S. Mission in this Caribbean Island nation. Knox was a military veteran, university educator, and career diplomat who served as U.S. Ambassador to Dahomey (now called Benin) from 1964 to 1969, and later to Haiti from 1969 to 1973.

November 14

1986 On this day in 1986, Ambassador Ronald Palmer presented his diplomatic credentials to the leadership in Mauritius, officially beginning his tenure in-residence as leader of the U.S. Mission in this this Sub-Saharan African island nation. Palmer was a career diplomat and university educator who served as a U.S. Ambassador on three occasions, including Togo from 1976 to 1978, Malaysia from 1981 to 1983, and Mauritius from 1986 to 1989.

November 15

1919 On this day in 1919, Samuel Westerfield was born in Chicago, Illinois. Westerfield was an economist, university educator, public servant, and diplomat who would serve as U.S. Ambassador to Liberia from 1969 to 1972.

1947 On this day in 1947, Elizabeth McKune was born in Detroit, Michigan. McKune, who was a career diplomat, would serve as U.S. Ambassador to Qatar from 1998 to 2001.

November 16

1999 On this day in 1999, President Bill Clinton nominated Harriet Elam-Thomas to be U.S. Ambassador to the Sub-Saharan African nation of Senegal and concurrently to Guinea-Bissau. Following Senate confirmation, Ambassador Elam-Thomas would serve as U.S. Ambassador to both of these nations until 2002.

November 17

1964 On this day in 1964, Susan Rice was born in Washington, DC. Rice was a Rhodes Scholar, foreign policy expert, and diplomat who served as U.S. Permanent Representative to the United Nations, with the rank of Ambassador, from 2009 to 2013.

November 18

1997 On this day in 1997, Ambassador George Moose presented his diplomatic credentials to the leadership of the European Office of the United Nations in Geneva (UN/Geneva), officially beginning his tenure in-residence as U.S. Permanent Representative to the (UN/Geneva), with the rank of Ambassador. He would serve in this role until 2001. Moose was a career diplomat who had also previously served as U.S. Ambassador to Benin from 1983 to 1986 and to Senegal from 1988 to 1991.

Major Milestone Moment

November 19

On this day in 2019, the podcast 80,000 Hours published the recording and transcript of its interview with **Ambassador Bonnie Jenkins**, where she discussed her years as Ambassador-At-Large responsible for coordinating the Department of State's global efforts to combat major security threats. In that work, she oversaw U.S. efforts to combat threats ranging from health security issues to nuclear issues to chemical weapons and more. Jenkins was a military veteran, international security and legal expert, and diplomat who served as the Department of State's Coordinator of Threat Reduction Programs, with the rank of Ambassador from 2009 to 2017.

November 20

2002 On this day in 2002, Ambassador Aurelia Brazeal presented her diplomatic credentials to the leadership in Ethiopia, officially beginning her tenure in-residence as the leader of the U.S. Mission in this Sub-Saharan African nation. Brazeal was a career diplomat who served as U.S. Ambassador on three (3) separate occasions, including Micronesia from 1990 to 1993, Kenya from 1993 to 1996, and Ethiopia from 2002 to 2005.

November 21

2011 On this day in 2011, Ambassador Nichole Avant officially ended her tenure as U.S. Ambassador to the Caribbean Island Nation of The Bahamas. Avant was an entertainment industry executive, fundraiser, and diplomat who served as U.S. Ambassador to the Bahamas from 2009 to 2011.

November 22

1993 On this day in 1993, President Bill Clinton nominated Leslie Alexander to be U.S. Ambassador to the Sub-Saharan African Island nation of Mauritius and concurrently to The Comoros. Following Senate confirmation, Ambassador Alexander would serve as U.S. Ambassador to both nations from 1993 to 1996. He would later also serve as U.S. Ambassador to Ecuador from 1996 to 1999.

November 23

1973 On this day in 1973, President Richard Nixon nominated O. Rudolph Aggrey to be U.S. Ambassador to Senegal and concurrently to The Gambia. Following Senate confirmation, Ambassador Aggrey, who was a university educator and diplomat, would serve as U.S. Ambassador to both Sub-Saharan African nations from 1973 to 1977. He would later also serve as U.S. Ambassador to Romania from 1977 to 1981.

November 24

1943 On this day in 1943, Aurelia Brazeal was born in Chicago, Illinois. Brazeal was a career diplomat who served as U.S. Ambassador on three separate occasions: Micronesia from 1990 to 1993; Kenya from 1993 to 1996; and Ethiopia from 2002 to 2005.

November 25

2013 On this day in 2013, Ambassador Pamela Bridgewater officially ended her tenure as U.S. Ambassador to Jamaica, where she had served since 2010. Bridgewater was a career diplomat and university educator who had earlier she had also served as U.S. Ambassador to Benin from 2000 to 2002 and to Ghana from 2005 to 2008.

November 26

2001 On this day in 2001, "The Washington Times" online, published an article entitled "Building Ties in Nigeria," which among other things, reported that U.S. Ambassador to Nigeria, Howard Jeter, had participated in a weekend meeting of the Nigeria-U.S. Joint Economic Partnership Committee in the Nigerian capital, Abuja, to explore ways to increase military and law enforcement cooperation in the wake of the September 11 terrorist attacks. Jeter was a career diplomat who had previously served as U.S. Ambassador to Botswana from 1993 to 1996 and was then serving as U.S. Ambassador to Nigeria from 2000 to 2003.

November 27

1997 On this day in 1997, Ambassador Jerome Cooper officially ended his tenure as U.S. Ambassador to Jamaica. Cooper was a military veteran, public servant, business leader, and diplomat who served as U.S. Ambassador to Jamaica from 1994 to 1997.

November 28

2021 On this day in 2021, the online website Healthcare Digital posted a list of the Top 10 influential healthcare leaders of that year, of which Dr. John Nkengasong was listed as number three (3). Dr. Nkengasong, at that time, was serving as the founding director of the Africa Centres for Disease Control and Prevention (Africa CDC). Late, in 2022, he would be appointed by U.S. President Joe Biden as Ambassador-at-Large with the title of Coordinator of United States Government Activities to Combat HIV/AIDS Globally. He was confirmed by the U.S. Senate for this ambassadorial rank and position in May of 2022.

Major Milestone Moment

November 29

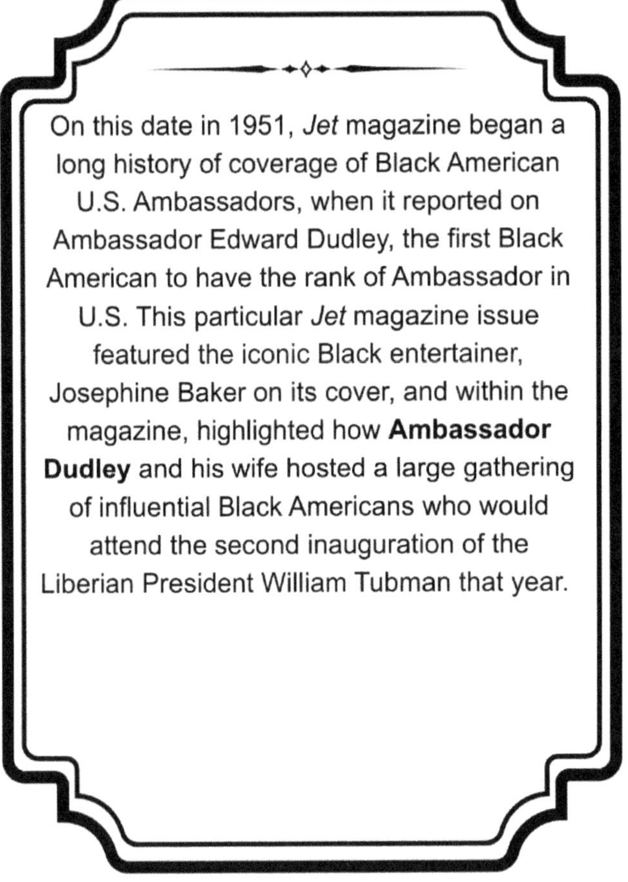

On this date in 1951, *Jet* magazine began a long history of coverage of Black American U.S. Ambassadors, when it reported on Ambassador Edward Dudley, the first Black American to have the rank of Ambassador in U.S. This particular *Jet* magazine issue featured the iconic Black entertainer, Josephine Baker on its cover, and within the magazine, highlighted how **Ambassador Dudley** and his wife hosted a large gathering of influential Black Americans who would attend the second inauguration of the Liberian President William Tubman that year.

November 30

2000 On this day in 2000, Ambassador George Staples, while leading the U.S. Mission in Rwanda, held a fundraiser event at the Ambassador's residence, designed to support the Kigali Public Library (KPL). The KPL was intended to be the country's first-ever national library open to all in a country that, less than a generation prior, had experienced a period of internal strife that was well known as "The Rwandan Genocide". Staples was a military veteran and career diplomat who served as U.S. Ambassador to Rwanda from 1998 to 2001, and later to Cameroon and Equatorial Guinea from 2001 to 2004.

CHAPTER 13:
DECEMBER

December 1

1981 On this day in 1981, President Ronald Reagan nominated Melvin Evans to be U.S. Ambassador to the Caribbean Island nation of Trinidad & Tobago. Following Senate confirmation, Ambassador Evans, a medical doctor, public servant, and diplomat, would serve as U.S. Ambassador in this nation until 1984.

Major Milestone Moment

December 2

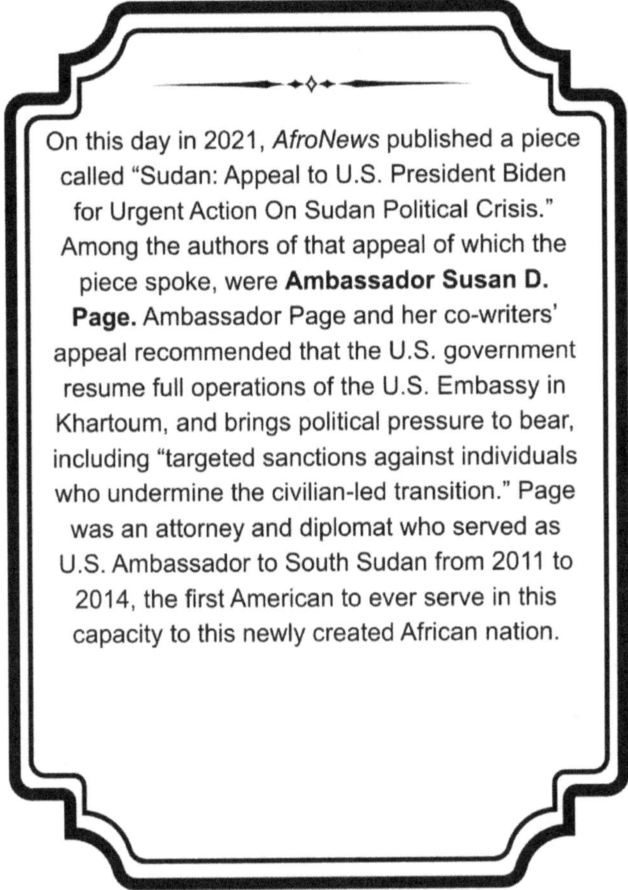

On this day in 2021, *AfroNews* published a piece called "Sudan: Appeal to U.S. President Biden for Urgent Action On Sudan Political Crisis." Among the authors of that appeal of which the piece spoke, were **Ambassador Susan D. Page.** Ambassador Page and her co-writers' appeal recommended that the U.S. government resume full operations of the U.S. Embassy in Khartoum, and brings political pressure to bear, including "targeted sanctions against individuals who undermine the civilian-led transition." Page was an attorney and diplomat who served as U.S. Ambassador to South Sudan from 2011 to 2014, the first American to ever serve in this capacity to this newly created African nation.

December 3

1935 On this day in 1935, Howard Walker was born in Newport News, Virginia. Walker was a military veteran and career diplomat who would serve as U.S. Ambassador to Togo from 1982 to 1984, and to Madagascar and The Comoros from 1989 to 1992.

December 4

2002 On this day in 2002, Ambassador Gail Mathieu presented her diplomatic credentials to the leadership in Niger, officially beginning her tenure in-residence as leader of the U.S. Mission to this Sub-Saharan African nation. Mathieu was an attorney and career diplomat who served as U.S. Ambassador to Niger from 2002 to 2005 and to Namibia from 2007 to 2010.

December 5

2001 On this day in 2001, Ambassador Francis Taylor, who was serving as the State Department's Coordinator for Counterterrorism with the rank of Ambassador-at-Large, began a two-day summit of talks with Chinese authorities on one of the few issues that China and the U.S. agreed on, which was that terrorism severely threatened the peace and development and the international community. The talks resulted in several comprehensive measures that the two nations agreed on to strike against any form of terrorism. Taylor was a military leader, intelligence and security expert, and diplomat who served as Coordinator of Counter-Terrorism and Director, Office to Monitor and Combat Trafficking in Persons, with rank of Ambassador from 2001 to 2004, and then later as Assistant Secretary, Bureau of Diplomatic Security and Director, Office of Foreign Missions, also with the rank of Ambassador from 2002 to 2005.

December 6

2001 On this day in 2001, Ambassador Roy Austin presented his diplomatic credentials to the leadership in Trinidad and Tobago, officially beginning his tenure in-residence as the leader of the U.S. Mission in this Caribbean Island nation. Austin was a university educator, scholar, and diplomat who served as U.S. Ambassador to Trinidad and Tobago from 2001 to 2009.

December 7

1956 On this day in 1956, Wanda Nesbitt was born in Philadelphia, Pennsylvania. Nesbitt was a career diplomat who served as U.S. Ambassador to three nations including Madagascar from 2001 to 2004; Côte d'Ivoire from 2007 to 2010; and Namibia from 2010 to 2013.

December 8

1992 On this day in 1992, Irvin Hicks, Sr., was confirmed by the U.S. Senate as Deputy Representative of the U.S. to the Security Council in the United Nations, with the rank of Ambassador. Hicks was a career diplomat who would serve as U.S. Ambassador on three (3) separate occasions including the Seychelles from 1985 to 1987, to the United Nations' Security Council with the rank of Ambassador from 1992 to 1993, and Ethiopia from 1994 to 1996.

December 9

1993 On this day in 1993, Ambassador Charles Baquet, III, officially ended his tenure as U.S. Ambassador to Djibouti. Baquet was a career diplomat who served as U.S. Ambassador to Djibouti from 1991 to 1993.

Major Milestone Moment

December 10

On this day in 2024, **Ambassador Jessica Davis Ba** was the subject of an article on the website ICSA Insight. The article, written by the youngest of her five sons, Soulayman Ba, is called "The Two Decade Long Journey of Jessica Davis Ba, U.S. Ambassador." It discusses her diplomatic career but also focuses on how she balanced that career with her family, including raising her five sons. Ambassador Davis Ba was a career diplomat who became the U.S. Ambassador to Côte d'Ivoire in 2022, and was still leading that U.S. Mission in 2025 at the time of writing.

December 10

2002 On this day in 2002, Ambassador Pamela Bridgewater officially ended her tenure as U.S. Ambassador to Benin. Bridgewater was a career diplomat and university educator who served as U.S. Ambassador on three (3) separate occasions, including Benin from 2000 to 2002, Jamaica from 2005 to 2008, and Jamaica from 2010 to 2013.

December 11

1976 On this day in 1976, Ambassador Charles James presented his diplomatic credentials to the leadership in Niger, officially beginning his tenure in-residence, as U.S. Ambassador to this Sub-Saharan African nation. James was a military veteran, attorney, public servant, and diplomat who served as U.S. Ambassador to Niger from 1976 to 1979.

December 12

1941 On this day in 1941, Charles Baquet III, born in New Orleans, Louisiana. Baquet was a career diplomat who would serve as U.S. Ambassador to Djibouti from 1991 to 1993.

December 13

2011 On this day in 2011, DEVEX published a photo of Sharon Cromer, then Acting Chief of the U.S. Agency for International Development (USAID) in Africa as she met with a small business owner in Johannesburg, as part of USAID's efforts to promote the important role of an effective and proactive private sector in boosting economic growth and wealth creation on the continent. In 2021, Cromer, a career diplomat and international development specialist, would be nominated by President Joe Biden as U.S. Ambassador to The Gambia. Following Senate confirmation in late 2021, she would be sworn in in early 2022 and then serve as U.S. Ambassador to The Gambia from that year until 2025.

December 14

2001 On this day in 2001, Ambassador Mattie R. Sharpless presented her diplomatic credentials to the leadership in the Central African Republic, receiving an official welcome and beginning her tenure as U.S. Ambassador to this Sub-Saharan African nation. Ambassador Sharpless would serve in this role until 2002. Ambassador Sharpless was a career member of the Foreign Agricultural Service (FAS) of the U.S. Department of Agriculture (USDA). In this role, she played a vital role in facilitating trade and international cooperation between other nations and the U.S., which were critical to the vitality of the U.S. agricultural sector. Sharpless was the first and only Black American to be appointed as an Ambassador from the ranks of the USDA/FAS.

December 15

1993 On this day in 1993, Ambassador Leslie Alexander presented his diplomatic credentials to the leadership in Mauritius, officially beginning his tenure in-residence, as U.S. Ambassador to this Sub-Saharan African island nation. He would simultaneously serve as U.S. Ambassador to the nearby islands of the Comoros. Alexander was a career diplomat who served as U.S. Ambassador to Mauritius and the Comoros from 1993 to 1996 and later to Ecuador from 1996 to 1999.

December 16

2016 On this day in 2016, Ambassador Patrick Gaspard officially ended his tenure as U.S. Ambassador to South Africa. Gaspard was a community and political organizer and diplomat who served as U.S. Ambassador to South Africa from 2013 to 2016.

December 17

2021 On this day in 2021, The Miami Student newspaper reported that the Miami (of Ohio) University Board of Trustees had voted to award Ambassador Sylvia Stanfield with an Honorary Doctor of Humane Letters degree at its upcoming fall commencement. Stanfield was a career diplomat who served as U.S. Ambassador to Brunei from 1999 to 2002.

December 18

1974 On this day in 1974, President Gerald Ford nominated Terence Todman to be U.S. Ambassador to Costa Rica. Following Senate confirmation, Todman would officially become U.S. Ambassador to this Central American nation, serving there until 1977. Ambassador Todman would become the Black American with the most ambassadorial appointments in history (six total). Prior to Costa Rica, he had served as U.S. Ambassador to Chad from 1969 to 1972 and to Guinea from 1972 to 1975. Following Costa Rica, he would serve in three more ambassadorial postings, including as U.S. Ambassador to Spain from 1978 to 1983, Denmark from 1983 to 1989, and Argentina from 1989 to 1993.

December 19

2014 On this day in 2014, President Barack Obama nominated Marcia Bernicat to be U.S. Ambassador to the South Asian nation of Bangladesh. Following Senate confirmation, Bernicat, a career diplomat, would go on to serve as U.S. Ambassador to Bangladesh from 2015 to 2018. She had previously also served as U.S. Ambassador to Senegal and concurrently to Guinea-Bissau from 2008 to 2011.

December 20

1996 On this day in 1996, Ambassador Arlene Render presented her diplomatic credentials to the leadership in Zambia, officially beginning her tenure in-residence, as leader of the U.S. Mission in this Sub-Saharan African nation. Render was a career diplomat who served as U.S. Ambassador on three (3) separate occasions, including The Gambia from 1990 to 1993, Zambia from 1996 to 1999, and Côte d'Ivoire from 2001 to 2004.

December 21

1893 On this day in 1893, Richard Jones was born in Albany, Georgia. Jones was a military veteran and leader who served in both World Wars, and a diplomat who would become only the third Black American ever appointed and served as U.S. Ambassador (to Liberia from 1955 to 1959).

December 22

2006 On this day in 2006, Ambassador Cindy Courville presented her diplomatic credentials to the leadership of the African Union (AU) in Addis Ababa, Ethiopia, officially beginning her tenure in-residence as leader of the U.S. Mission to this African body. Courville, an African scholar and expert, and diplomat who served as U.S. Representative to the African Union (AU), with the rank of Ambassador from 2006 to 2008. She was the first ever U.S. Ambassador to this body as well as the first ever Ambassador from a non-African state.

December 23

1923 On this day in 1923, David Bolen was born in Heflin, Louisiana. Bolen would become a military veteran, athlete, Olympian, and diplomat who would serve as U.S. Ambassador to Botswana, Lesotho, and Swaziland from 1974 to 1976, and to the German Democratic Republic, then popularly known as communist East Germany, from 1977 to 1980. While serving as Ambassador in East Germany, Bolen played a critical role in helping the U.S. promote better relations, including through trade, between East and West Germany. Ultimately, the Berlin Wall separating the nations and ushering in a democratic government and unified Germany would happen in 1989, and Ambassador Bolen's efforts certainly helped lay some of the groundwork for this significant moment in world history.

December 24

1992 On this day in 1992, Ambassador Ruth Davis presented her diplomatic credentials to the leadership in

Benin, officially beginning her tenure as U.S. Ambassador to this Sub-Saharan African nation. A career diplomat, Ambassador Davis would serve as U.S. Ambassador to Benin until 1995. She later became the first Black American to serve as Director of the Foreign Service Institute, where she did so from 1997 to 2001; and the first Black American female to serve as Director General of the Foreign Service, which she did from 2001 to 2003.

December 25

2018 On this day in 2018, the *Hamilton News* and online news source of Hamilton College in Clinton, New York, published its top ten events of the year. Among those events highlighted was a high-level foreign policy discussion held on the campus earlier that year, featuring Dr. Susan Rice, former U.S. Ambassador to the United Nations and National Security Advisor to President Barack Obama, and Dr. Condoleezza Rice, former Secretary of State and National Security Advisor to President George W. Bush. The discussion covered a number of key global topics, but it was noted in the original article about the event (in April of 2018) how "while their opinions differed, Rice and Rice never lost the air of mutual respect that provided the foundation for an engaging and constructive discussion about hot-button issues facing the United States today."

December 26

2014 On this day in 2014, Ambassador Cynthia Akuetteh presented her diplomatic credentials to the leadership in Gabon, officially beginning her tenure as leader of the U.S. Mission in this Sub-Saharan African nation. She would concurrently serve as U.S. Ambassador to São Tomé & Principe. Akuetteh was a career diplomat who served as U.S. Ambassador to Gabon and concurrently to São Tomé and Principe from 2014 to 2018.

December 27

2018 On this day in 2018, the online news source *Pindula*, reported that Ambassador Brian Nichols, who was serving as U.S. Ambassador to Zimbabwe at the time, had informed the Zimbabwean government. Furthermore, the U.S. had set aside approximately $230 million in its foreign affairs budget for Zimbabwe for various sectors of the economy, which included health, targeting the mitigation of cholera, and HIV. He also stated that American businesses had regularly been contacting the U.S. Embassy about investment opportunities in the country. Ambassador Nichols was a career diplomat who served as U.S. Ambassador to Peru from 2014 to 2017, prior to his role as U.S. Ambassador to Zimbabwe beginning in 2018.

December 28

2000 On this day in 2000, President Bill Clinton nominated Howard Jeter to be U.S. Ambassador to Nigeria. Following Senate confirmation, Ambassador Jeter would serve as U.S. Ambassador to this Sub-Saharan African nation until 2003. Jeter was a career diplomat, and he had also previously served as U.S. Ambassador to Botswana from 1993 to 1996.

December 29

1967 On this day in 1967, Ambassador Hugh Smythe presented his diplomatic credentials to the leadership of Malta, officially beginning his tenure as leader of the U.S. Mission in this European nation. Smythe was a military veteran, university educator, scholar, and diplomat who served as U.S. Ambassador to Syria from 1965 to 1967, making him the first-ever Black American to be an Ambassador in the Middle East; as well as U.S. Ambassador to Malta from 1967 to 1969.

Major Milestone Moment

December 30

On this day in 1979, *The Washington Post* printed an online article that discussed the U.S. efforts to obtain a United Nations (UN) Security Council vote on sanctions against Iran, following the capture of hostages during the period known as the Iran Hostage Crisis. The article noted that the lobbying efforts led by U.S. Ambassador to the UN, **Donald McHenry**, and the U.S. Secretary of State to get the Security Council votes for those sanctions were a difficult one for the U.S. leadership. Donald McHenry was a scholar, corporate governor, university educator, and diplomat who served as U.S. Permanent Representative to the UN with the rank of Ambassador from 1979 to 1981. He would also later join the Board of the Coca-Cola Company (1981), making him the first Black American Board Member of this major global corporation.

December 31

1947 On this day in 1947, Richard Baltimore was born in New York, New York. Baltimore was an attorney and career diplomat who would serve as U.S. Ambassador to Oman from 2002 to 2006.

CHAPTER 14:
CONCLUSION

As this book concludes, it is important to emphasize that it should not be seen as a loose collection of random dates, months, or facts. Instead, it provides further evidence that Black people make history every day—even in areas of society that often receive little attention. Too often, education and recognition of Black achievements center on athletes, entertainers, politicians, and other figures who gain mainstream visibility. In contrast, fields such as foreign and diplomatic affairs receive far less acknowledgment, despite the profound contributions of Black Americans who have held leadership roles there. This is one of the central reasons why this text has focused on one particular leadership role through which history has been and continues to be made by Black Americans: the U.S. Ambassador.

Another reason this book represents an important addition to Black history is that, for many, Black historical moments are not part of everyday thought. Most—but unfortunately not all—Americans commemorate Black History Month in February. Each January, we honor the birth of Dr. Martin Luther King Jr., one of the most iconic leaders of the Civil Rights Movement. Juneteenth is increasingly recognized as a time to celebrate the end of slavery in the United States in 1865, when the last enslaved people were freed in Galveston, Texas. Many also mark Kwanzaa each December, celebrating African American culture through its seven principles. These events are vital milestones that highlight Black contributions, culture, and triumphs. Yet, given the countless ways Black Americans have shaped both U.S. and global history, we must continually elevate more stories. This book seeks to do just that by spotlighting the lives and milestones of Black U.S. Ambassadors.

As shown here, at least one future Black American who would go on to become a U.S. Ambassador was born in every month of the year. These Ambassadors presented credentials to, and regularly engaged with, key world leaders, including African independence figures like Jomo Kenyatta of Kenya (Ambassador William LeMelle) and global icons like Nelson Mandela of South Africa (Ambassador James Joseph). They influenced events tied to some of the most consequential moments in U.S. and world history: the Civil Rights Movement (Ambassadors Andrew Young, Ambassador Franklin Williams, and others), the Iran Hostage Crisis (Ambassador Ulric Haynes), the Rwandan Genocide (Ambassador Pierre-Richard Prosper), the Anti-Apartheid Movement in South Africa (multiple Ambassadors), the fall of the Berlin Wall (Ambassador David Bolen); and many others.

This book demonstrates that there are countless untold stories and milestones involving Black American leaders. It is the first to focus on these leaders both individually and collectively in their role as U.S. Ambassadors. It is meant to spark greater recognition, dialogue, and research into the critical contributions of Black Ambassadors to American and world history.

The evidence presented here illustrates that Black Americans—particularly those appointed as Ambassadors—have held influential leadership roles in shaping U.S. foreign policy and diplomacy, fields where Black voices are often perceived as muted or absent. Their impact has extended domestically as well, shaping pivotal moments in U.S. history before, during, and after their ambassadorships. These individuals, entrusted by the President of the United States to represent the nation abroad, embody stories that are both educational and inspirational. Though only 166 Black Americans have attained the rank and title of Ambassador, their collective influence speaks volumes about their resilience, leadership, and lasting contributions to national and global affairs.

As the pages of this book close, there are two truths to carry forward and repeat often:

Black History is Made Every Day.

Black History is American History.

INDEX

INDEX: BLACK AMBASSADOR FIRSTS (NOT EXHAUSTIVE)		
	Milestone	**Name and Country/International Organization/Posting and year of appointment as U.S. Ambassador…**
First	Black American to pass the U.S. Department of State's Foreign Service Officer Exam (1929)	Clifton R. Wharton, Sr. (Norway, 1961)
First	Black American U.S. Ambassador	Edward R. Dudley (Liberia, 1949)
First	Issue of *Jet* magazine that included coverage of a Black Ambassador (Edward Dudley). November 29, 1951 issue.	Edward R. Dudley (Liberia, 1949)
First	Black American Woman Ambassador	Patricia R. Harris (Luxembourg, 1965)
First	U.S. Ambassador to Guinea	John H. Morrow (Guinea, 1959)
First	Black American Ambassador appointed to a European nation	Clifton R. Wharton, Sr. (Norway, 1961)
First	Black American appointed U.S. Ambassador on multiple occasions	Mercer Cook (Niger, 1961; Senegal, 1964; The Gambia, 1965)
First	Black American husband-wife to serve as U.S. Ambassadors	Hugh H. Smythe (Syria, 1965; Malta 1967) and Mabel M. Smythe (Cameroon, 1977; Equatorial Guinea, 1979)
First	Black American appointed U.S. Ambassador to a country in the Middle East	Hugh H. Smythe (Syria, 1965)

First	Black female cabinet minister in the federal government (1977, Secretary of the Department of Housing and Urban Development under Jimmy Carter)	Patricia R. Harris (Luxembourg, 1965)
First	Black Mayor of a major U.S. City (Cleveland, 1967)	Carl B. Stokes (Seychelles, 1994)
First	Black American to be appointed as an Assistant Secretary of States (for Security and Consular Affairs, 1968)	Barbara M. Watson (Malaysia, 1980)
First	U.S. Ambassador to the Federated States of Micronesia	Aurelia E. Brazeal (Micronesia, 1990)
First	Black woman Foreign Service Officer to rise from the entry level of the Service to its Senior Ranks.	Aurelia E. Brazeal (Micronesia, 1990; Kenya, 1993; Ethiopia, 2002)
First	Black American to lead a Marine riflemen unit into combat (1966)	Jerome Gary Cooper (Jamaica, 1994)
First	Black American to play football at Cornell University (1935)	Jerome H. Holland (Sweden, 1970)
First	Black American to sit on the Board of the U.S. Stock Exchange (1972)	Jerome H. Holland (Sweden, 1970)
First	U.S. Ambassador to Swaziland after it became independent from Britain (1966)	Charles J. Nelson (Swaziland, 1971)
First	Black American to serve as U.S. Ambassador to a country in the Caribbean	Theadore Britton (Barbados and Grenada, 1974)
First	Black American to serve as U.S. Ambassador to the United Nations (UN)	Andrew Young (United Nations, 1977)
First	Black American to serve as U.S. Ambassador to a country in the East Asian and Pacific region of the world	Maurice Bean (Burma, 1977)
First	Black American to be appointed as a U.S. Ambassador-At-Large	William Beverly Carter (At-Large, Liaison with State and Local Government, 1977)
First	Black American to be promoted to rank of Career Ambassador; the Department of State's equivalent to a Four-Star General (October 17, 1989)	Terence Todman (Chad, 1969; Guinea, 1982; Costa Rica, 1974; Denmark, 1983)

First	And ONLY U.S. Ambassador to present credentials to, and serve during the Nelson Mandela Presidency in South Africa	James A. Joseph (South African, 1995)
First	Black American mayor of a major city (Cleveland, Ohio: 1967–1971)	Carl B. Stokes (The Seychelles, 1994)
First	Black American woman U.S. Senator (from 1993 – 1998 for the state of Illinois)	Carol Moseley Braun (New Zealand, 1999; Samoa, 2000)
First	Black American to serve as Director General of the U.S. Foreign Service (1989)	Edward Perkins (Liberia, 1985; South Africa, 1986; United Nations, 1992; Australia, 1993)
First	Black woman to be promoted to the rank of Career Ambassador; the Department of State's equivalent to a Four-Star General (May 1, 2002)	Ruth Davis (Benin, 1992)
First	Black American to serve as U.S. Ambassador to a country in the South and Central Asian region	Harry K. Thomas, Jr. (Bangladesh, 2003)
First	American woman to lead a U.S. consulate, as Counsel General, in the gender conservative Kingdom of Saudia Arabia (2002 to 2004)	Gina Abercrombie-Winstanley (Malta, 2012)
First	U.S. Ambassador to the African Union	Cindy L. Courville (African Union, 2006)
First	U.S. Ambassador to South Sudan	Susan D. Page (South Sudan, 2011)

INDEX: FULL LIST OF BLACK AMERICAN U.S. AMBASSADORS (1949-Present) By Year of Appointment 166 Total: 109 Living 66%; 57 deceased (34%)		
Year	**Name**	**Country/Posting (Dates)**
1949	Edward R. Dudley* (NCA)	Liberia (1949-1953)
1950	NONE	
1951	NONE	
1952	NONE	
1953	Jesie D. Locker* (NCA)	Liberia (1953-1955)
1954	NONE	
1955	Richard L. Jones* (NCA)	Liberia (1955-1959)
1956	NONE	
1957	NONE	
1958	NONE	
1959	John H. Morrow* (NCA)	Guinea (1959-1961)
1960	NONE	
1961	Clifton R. Wharton, Sr.* (FSO)	Norway (1961-1964)
	Will Mercer Cook* (NCA)	Niger (1961-1964)
1962	NONE	
1963	Carl T. Rowan* (NCA)	Finland (1963-1964)
1964	Clinton E. Knox* (FSO)	Dahomey (1964-1969)
	Will Mercer Cook* (NCA)	Senegal & The Gambia (1964-1966)
1965	Patricia Roberts Harris* (NCA)	Luxembourg (1965-1967)
	Hugh H. Smythe* (NCA)	Syria (1965-1968)
	Franklin H. Williams* (NCA)	Ghana (1965-1968)
1966	Elliot P. Skinner* (NCA)	Upper Volta (1966-1969)
1967	Hugh H. Smythe* (NCA)	Malta (1967-1969)
1968	Samuel C. Adams* (NCA)	Niger (1968-1969)
1969	Terence A. Todman* (FSO)	Chad (1969-1972)
	Samuel Z. Westerfield* (FSO)	Liberia (1969-1972)
	Clinton E. Knox* (FSO)	Haiti (1969-1973)
1970	Jerome H. Holland* (NCA)	Sweden (1970-1972)
	Clarence C. Ferguson, Jr. * (NCA)	Uganda (1970-1972)

1971	Charles J. Nelson* (NCA)	Botswana, Lesotho, and Swaziland (1971-1974)
	John E. Reinhardt* (FSO)	Nigeria (1971-1975)
1972	William B. Carter* (FSO)	Tanzania (1972-1975)
	Terence A. Todman * (FSO)	Guinea (1972-1975)
1973	O. Rudolph Aggrey* (FSO)	Senegal and The Gambia (1973-1977)
1974	David B. Bolen* (FSO)	Botswana, Lesotho, and Swaziland (1974-1976)
	Theodore R. Britton, Jr. (NCA)	Barbados and Grenada (1974-1976)
	Terence A. Todman	Costa Rica (1974-1977)
1975	NONE	
1976	Ronald D. Palmer* (FSO)	Togo (1976-1978)
	William B. Carter* (FSO)	Liberia (1976-1979)
	Charles A. James* (NCA)	Niger (1976-1979
1977	Andrew J. Young (NCA)	USUN/ New York (1977-1979)
	Maurice D. Bean* (FSO)	Burma (1977-1979)
	Richard K. Fox, Jr.* (FSO)	Trinidad and Tobago (1977-1979)
	Mabel M. Smythe (NCA)	Cameroon (1977-1980)
	William B. Jones* (FSO)	Haiti (1977-1980)
	Wilbert J. LeMelle* (NCA)	Kenya & The Seychelles (1977-1980)
	David B. Bolen*(FSO)	East Germany (1977-1980)
	Ulric S. Haynes, Jr.* (NCA)	Algeria (1977-1981)
	O. Rudolph Aggrey* (FSO)	Romania (1977-1981)
1978	Terence A. Todman* (FSO)	Spain (1978-1983)
1979	Mabel M. Smythe* (NCA)	Equatorial Guinea (1979-1980)
	Donald F. McHenry (NCA)	USUN/ New York (1979-1981)
	Horace G. Dawson (FSO)	Botswana (1979-1981)
	Anne F. Holloway* (NCA)	Mali (1979-1981)

	William B. Carter* (FSO)	At-Large (Liaison w/ State & Local Gov't) (1979-1981)
1980	Barbara M. Watson* (NCA)	Malaysia (1980-1981)
	Walter C. Carrington* (NCA)	Senegal (1980-1981)
1981	Gerald E. Thomas* (NCA)	Guyana (1981-1983)
	John A. Burroughs, Jr. * (NCA)	Malawi (1981-1984)
	Ronald D. Palmer* (FSO)	Malaysia (1981-1984)
	Melvin H. Evans* (NCA)	Trinidad and Tobago (1981-1984)
1982	Howard K. Walker* (FSO)	Togo (1982-1984)
1983	Arthur W. Lewis* (FSO)	Sierra Leone (1983-1986)
	Gerald E. Thomas* (NCA)	Kenya (1983-1989)
	George E. Moose (FSO)	Benin (1983-1986)
	Terence A. Todman* (FSO)	Denmark (1983-1989)
1984	NONE	
1985	Edward J. Perkins* (FSO)	Liberia (1985-1986)
	Irvin Hicks, Sr. (FSO)	The Seychelles (1985-1987)
1986	Ronald D. Palmer* (FSO)	Mauritius (1986-1989)
	Cynthia Shepard Perry* (FSO)	Sierra Leone (1986-1989)
	Edward J. Perkins* (FSO)	South Africa (1986-1989)
1987	NONE	
1988	Leonard H. O. Spearman, Sr.* (NCA)	Rwanda (1988-1990)
	George E. Moose (FSO)	Senegal (1988-1991)
	John A. Burroughs, Jr.* (NCA)	Uganda (1988-1991)
1989	Ruth V. Washington** (NCA)	The Gambia (1989)
	Howard K. Walker* (FSO)	Madagascar & The Comoros (1989-1992)
	Johnny Young* (FSO)	Sierra Leone (1989-1992)
	Cynthia Shepard Perry* (NCA)	Burundi (1989-1993)
	Terence A. Todman* (FSO)	Argentina (1989-1993)

	Jewel Stradford Lafontant* (NCA)	At-Large (U.S. Coordinator for Refugee Affairs) (1989-1993)
1990	J. Steven Rhodes (NCA)	Zimbabwe (1990)
	Aurelia Erskine Brazeal (FSO)	Micronesia (1990-1993)
	Arlene Render (FSO)	The Gambia (1990-1993
	Leonard H. O. Spearman, Sr.* (NCA)	Lesotho (1990-1993)
1991	Charles R. Baquet, III (FSO)	Djibouti (1991-1993)
	Johnnie Carson (FSO)	Uganda 1991-1994)
1992	Edward J. Perkins* (FSO)	USUN/ New York (1992-1993)
	Irvin Hicks, Sr. (FSO)	Alternate Representative of the U.S. to the 47th Session of the General Assembly of the United Nations (With Rank of Ambassador) (1992-1993)
	Ruth A. Davis* (FSO)	Benin (1992-1995)
	Kenton Wesley Keith (FSO)	Qatar (1992-1995)
	Joseph Monroe Segars* (FSO)	Cape Verde (1992-1996)
1993	Aurelia Erskine Brazeal (FSO)	Kenya (1993-1996)
	Edward J. Perkins* (FSO)	Australia (1993-1996)
	Leslie M. Alexander (FSO)	Mauritius & The Comoros (1993-1996)
	Howard F. Jeter (FSO)	Botswana (1993-1996)
	Walter C. Carrington* (NCA)	Nigeria (1993-1997)
1994	Carl B. Stokes* (NCA)	The Seychelles (1994-1995)
	Irvin Hicks, Sr. (FSO)	Ethiopia (1994-1996)
	Johnny Young* (FSO)	Togo (1994-1997)
	Jerome G. Cooper* (NCA)	Jamaica (1994-1997)
	Sidney Williams (NCA)	Bahamas (1994-1998)
1995	Johnnie Carson (FSO)	Zimbabwe (1995-1997)

	Mosina H. Jordan (FSO)	Central African Republic (1995-1997)
	Bismark Myrick* (FSO)	Lesotho (1995-1998)
	James A. Joseph* (NCA)	South Africa (1995-1999)
1996	Leslie M. Alexander (FSO)	Ecuador (1996-1999)
	John F. Hicks, Sr.* (FSO)	Eritrea (1996-1997)
	Arlene Render (FSO)	Zambia (1996-1999)
	Sharon P. Wilkinson (FSO)	Burkina Faso (1996-1999)
1997	Bernda Schoonover	Togo (1997-2000)
	Betty E. King (NCA)	USUN/ECOSOC (1997-2001)
	George E. Moose (FSO)	USUN/Geneva (1997-2001)
	Johnny Young* (FSO)	Bahrain (1997-2001)
1998	Shirley E. Barnes (FSO)	Madagascar (1998-2001)
	William D. Clarke (FSO)	Eritrea (1998-2001)
	George W. B. Haley* (NCA)	The Gambia (1998-2001)
	Elizabeth D. McKune (FSO)	Qatar (1998-2001)
	Robert C. Perry (FSO)	Central African Republic (1998-2001)
	George M. Staples (FSO)	Rwanda (1998-2001)
	Charles R. Stith (NCA)	Tanzania (1998-2001)
1999	Carol Moseley-Braun (NCA)	New Zealand & Samoa (1999-2001)
	Diane E. Watson NCA)	Micronesia (1999-2001)
	Gregory L. Johnson (FSO)	Swaziland (1999-2001)
	Delano Eugene Lewis, Sr.* (NCA)	South Africa (1999-2001)
	Harriet L. Elam-Thomas (FSO)	Senegal (1999-2002)
	Bismark Myrick* (FSO)	Liberia (1999-2002)
	Sylvia Gaye Stanfield (FSO)	Brunei Darussalam (1999-2002)
	Johnnie Carson (FSO)	Kenya (1999-2003)
2000	Pamela E. Bridgewater (FSO)	Benin (2000-2002)
	Sharon P. Wilkinson (FSO)	Mozambique (2000-2003)

	Howard F. Jeter (FSO)	Nigeria (2000-2003)
2001	Mattie R. Sharpless (FSO)	Central African Republic (2001-2002)
	George M. Staples (FSO)	Cameroon/Equatorial Guinea (2001-2004)
	Arlene Render (FSO)	Cote d'Ivoire (2001-2004)
	Johnny Young* (FSO)	Slovenia (2001-2004)
	Francis X. Taylor (NCA)	At-Large: Coordinator of Counter-Terrorism and Director, Office to Monitor and Combat Trafficking in Persons (2001-2004)
	Wanda L. Nesbitt (FSO)	Madagascar (2001-2004)
	Pierre-Richard Prosper (NCA)	At-Large (Office of War Crimes) (2001-2005)
	Roy L. Austin (NCA)	Trinidad and Tobago (2001-2009)
2002	James D. McGee (FSO)	Swaziland (2002-2004)
	Larry L. Palmer* (FSO)	Honduras (2002-2005)
	Joseph Huggins (FSO)	Botswana (2002-2005)
	James I. Gadsden (FSO)	Iceland (2002-2005)
	Aurelia E. Brazeal (FSO)	Ethiopia (2002-2005)
	Robin R. Sanders (FSO)	Congo (2002-2005)
	Charles A. Ray (FSO)	Cambodia (2002-2005)
	Gail Denise Mathieu (FSO)	Níger (2002-2005)
	Francis X. Taylor (NCA)	Assistant Secretary, Bureau of Diplomatic Security & Director, Office of Foreign Missions (with Rank of Ambassador) (2002-2005)
	Richard L. Baltimore (FSO)	Oman (2002-2006)
2003	Harry K. Thomas, Jr. (FSO)	Bangladesh (2003-2005)
	Roland W. Bullen (FSO)	Guyana (2003-2006)

2004	Jendayi E. Frazer (NCA)	South Africa (2004-2005)
	Margarita D. Ragsdale (FSO)	Djibouti (2004-2006)
	June Carter Perry (FSO)	Lesotho (2004-2007)
	Joyce A. Barr (FSO)	Namibia (2004-2007)
	James D. McGee (FSO)	Madagascar & The Comoros (2004-2007)
2005	Roger D. Pierce (FSO)	Cape Verde (2005-2007)
	Pamela E. Bridgewater (FSO)	Ghana (2005-2008)
2006	Cindy L. Courville (NCA)	African Union (2006-2008)
	Clyde Bishop (FSO)	Marshall Islands (2006-2008)
	Eric M. Bost (NCA)	South Africa (2006-2009)
	Gayleatha B. Brown* FSO)	Benin (2006-2009)
	Bernadette M. Allen (FSO)	Niger (2006-2010)
2007	Barry L. Wells (NCA)	The Gambia (2007-2009)
	James D. McGee (FSO)	Zimbabwe (2007-2009)
	Maurice S. Parker (FSO)	Swaziland (2007-2009)
	June Carter Perry (FSO)	Sierra Leone (2007-2009)
	Gail D. Mathieu (FSO)	Namibia (2007-2010)
	John L. Withers (FSO)	Albania (2007-2010)
	Eunice S. Reddick (FSO)	Gabon & Sao Tome and Principe (2007-2010)
	Wanda L. Nesbitt (FSO)	Cote d'Ivoire (2007-2010)
	Robin R. Sanders (FSO)	Nigeria (2007-2010)
2008	John M. Jones (FSO)	Guyana (2008-2009)
	Marcia S. Bernicat (FSO)	Senegal and Guinea Bissau (2008-2011)
	C. Steven McGann* (FSO)	Fiji, Kiribati, Nauru, Tonga, and Tuvalu (2008-2011)
	Linda Thomas-Greenfield (FSO)	Liberia (2008-2012)
2009	Gayleatha Brown* (FSO)	Burkina Faso (2009)

	Nicole A. Avant (NCA)	Bahamas (2009-2011)
	Charles A. Ray (FSO)	Zimbabwe (2009-2012)
	Teddy B. Taylor (FSO)	Papua New Guinea, Solomon Islands, and Vanuatu (2009-2012)
	Susan E. Rice (NCA)	USUN/ New York (2009-2013)
	Ron Kirk (NCA)	U.S. Trade Representative (with Rank of Ambassador) (2009-2013)
	Michael A. Battle (NCA)	African Union (2009-2013)
	Alfonso E. Lenhardt (NCA)	Tanzania (2009-2013)
	Bonnie D. Jenkins (NCA)	Coordinator for Thread Reduction Programs (with Rank of Ambassador) (2009-2017)
	Ertharin Cousins (NCA)	USUN/Rome (2009-2017)
2010	Mary Jo Wills (FSO)	Mauritius and The Seychelles (2010-2011)
	Beatrice Welters (NCA)	Trinidad and Tobago (2010-2012)
	William Kennard (NCA)	European Union (2010-2013)
	Wanda L. Nesbitt (FSO)	Namibia (2010-2013)
	Betty E. King (NCA)	USUN/Geneva (2010-2013)
	Harry K. Thomas, Jr. (FSO)	Philippines (2010-2013)
	Bisa Williams (FSO)	Niger (2010-2013)
	Helen Reed-Rowe* (FSO)	Palau (2010-2013)
	Pamela Bridgewater (FSO)	Jamaica (2010-2013)
2011	Suzan Johnson Cook (NCA)	At-Large (International Religious Freedom) (2011-2013)
	Pamela L. Spratlen (FSO)	Republic of Kyrgyzstan (2011-2014)

	Susan D. Page (NCA)	South Sudan (2011-2014)
	Sue K. Brown* (FSO)	Montenegro (2011-2015)
	Frankie A. Reed (FSO)	Fiji, Kiribati, Nauru, Tonga, and Tuvalu (2011-2015)
	Adrienne S. O'Neal (FSO)	Cape Verde (2011-2015)
2012	Makila James (FSO)	Swaziland (2012-2015)
	Larry L. Palmer* (FSO)	Barbados, St. Kitts and Nevis (East Caribbean, & the Organization of Eastern Caribbean States) (2012-2016)
	Gina Abercrombie-Winstanley (FSO)	Malta (2012-2016)
2013	Reuben E. Brigety, II (NCA)	African Union (2013-2015)
	Tulinabo S. Mushingi (FSO)	Burkina Faso (2013-2016)
	Patrick H. Gaspard (NCA)	South Africa (2013-2016)
2014	Dwight L. Bush, Sr. (NCA)	Morocco (2014-2017)
	Michael A. Lawson (NCA)	International Civil Aviation Organization (2014-2017)
	Brian Nichols (FSO)	Peru (2014-2017)
	Eunice S. Reddick (FSO)	Niger (2014-2017)
	Todd D. Robinson (FSO)	Guatemala (2014-2017)
	Daniel W. Yohannes (NCA)	Organization for Economic Cooperation and Development (OECD) (2014-2017)
	Crystal Nix-Hines (NCA)	United Nations Educational, Scientific, and Cultural Organization (UNESCO) (2014-2017)

	Cynthia H. Akuetteh (FSO)	Gabon & Sao Tome and Principe (2014-2018)
	Pamela L. Spratlen(FSO)	Uzbekistan (2014-2018)
	Marcia S. Bernicat (FSO)	Bangladesh (2014-2018)
	Robert A. Wood (FSO)	U.S. Representative to the Conference on Disarmament and U.S. Special Representative for Biological & Toxin Weapons Convention Issues (With Rank of Ambassador) (2014-2020)
2015	Gentry O. Smith (FSO)	Director of the Office of Foreign Missions (with Ambassador Rank) (2015-2017)
	Stafford Fitzgerald Haney (NCA)	Costa Rica (2015-2017)
	Carolyn P. Alsup (FSO)	The Gambia (2015-2018)
	Harry K. Thomas, Jr. (FSO)	Zimbabwe (2015-2018)
2016	John L. Estrada (NCA)	Trinidad & Tobago (2016-2017)
2017	Tulinabo S. Mushingi (FSO)	Senegal & Guinea-Bissau (2017-2021)
2018	Joel E. Danies (FSO)	Gabon & Sao Tome and Principe (2018- 2019)
	Dereck J. Hogan (FSO)	Moldova (2018-2021)
	Brian A. Nichols (FSO)	Zimbabwe (2018-2021)
2019	Natalie E. Brown (FSO)	Uganda (2019-2023)
2020	NONE	
2021	Linda Thomas-Greenfield (FSO)	USUN/New York (2021-2025)
	Michael A. Battle (NCA)	Tanzania (2021-2025)
	Sharon L. Cromer (FSO)	The Gambia (2021-2025)

	Tulinabo S, Mushingi (FSO)	Angola & Sao Tome and Principe (2021-2025)
	N. Nickolas Perry (NCA)	Jamaica (2021-2025)
2022	Yohannes Abraham (NCA)	Representative of the United States of America to the Association of Southeast Asian Nations (ASEAN) (With Rank of Ambassador) (2022-2025)
	Jessica Davis Ba (FSO)	Cote d'Ivoire (2022-2025) still on duty as of 11//25
	Candace A. Bond (NCA)	Trinidad and Tobago (2022-2025)
	Reuben E. Brigety, II (NCA)	South Africa (2022-2025)
	Timmy T. Davis (FSO)	Qatar (2022-2025)
	John Nkengasong (NCA)	Coordinator of United States Government Activities to Combat HIV/AIDS Globally (With Rank of Ambassador-At Large) (2022-2025)
	Robert A. Wood (FSO)	Representative of the United States of America to the Association of Southeast Asian Nations (ASEAN) (With Rank of Ambassador) (2022-2025)
2023	Vernelle Trim FitzPatrick (FSO)	Gabon (2023-2025) still on duty as of 11/25
	Ervin J. Massinga (FSO)	Ethiopia (2023-2025) still on duty as of 11/25
2024	Arthur W. Brown (FSO)	Ecuador (2004- 2025)

NCA = Non Career Appointees
FSO = Foreign Service Officers
*Deceased
**Tragically, Ambassador Washington was killed in a car accident in January of 1990, in the United States, just one week prior to her departure to serve as U.S. Ambassador in The Gambia.

BIBLIOGRAPHY

African American Registry Website. Accessed at: https://aaregistry.org/story/educator-and-diplomat-jerome-holland/ on 9/11/2025

Afro American. 1986. "Four Black Women Appointed United States Ambassadors" in *Washington Afro-American,* October 28,

Anderson, Carol. 1996. "From Hope to Disillusion: African Americans, the United Nations, and the Struggle for Human Rights, 1944-1947," *Diplomatic History,* Fall: 531-563

Anderson, Carol. 2003. *Eyes Off the Prize: The United Nations and the African American Struggle for Human Rights*, 1944-1955. Cambridge: Cambridge University Press

Bridgewater, Pamela. 2025. *Bridging Troubled Waters: A Memoir*. BK Royston Publishing

Dandridge, James. 2014. "Remembering a Born Diplomat and Consummate Professional." *The Foreign Service Journal,* November: 63

Davis, Ruth. 2008. "Distinguished African Americans at the Department of States," U.S. Department of State FY2008 Financial Report, Bureau of Management. Retrieved February 14, 2012 (http://www.state.gov/s/d/rm/rls/perfrpt/2008/html/112148.htm)

Dawson, Horace. 1993. "First African-American Diplomat." *Foreign Service Journal,* January: 42

Foreign Service Journal. 2014. "In Memory Section," *Foreign Service Journal,* November 2014. Retrieved November 23, 2014 (http://www.afsa.org/FSJ/1114/files/assets/basic-html/page86.html)

Heinl, Nancy. 1973. "America's First Black Diplomat," *Foreign Service Journal,* August: 20-22

Hevesi, Dennis. 2007. "Elliott Skinner, Scholar and Former Ambassador, dies at 82," *The New York Times,* May 1

Janken, Kenneth. 2003. "Making Racial Change, Managing Racial Change: The Civil Rights Movement, U.S. Foreign Policy, and Race RelationsOn the World Stage," *Diplomatic History* 27, 5: 717-723

Johnson, Benita. 2007. "African-Americans and American Foreign Policy." *Journal of Pan African Studies,* 1, 8: 33-51

Justesen, Benjamin. 2004. "African-American Consuls Abroad, 1897-1909," *Foreign Service Journal,* September: 72-76

Keeley, Robert. 2000. *First Line of Defense: Ambassadors, Embassies, and American Interests Abroad.* Washington, D.C.: The American Academy of Diplomacy

Krenn, Michael. 1998. *Black Diplomacy: African Americans and the State Department*, 1945 – 1969. New York: M.E. Sharpe Publisher

McLellan, Carlton E. 2018. "Black American Ambassadors: Milestones in Diplomatic & Exchange Leadership" in *Exchange Matters,* newsletter of *Global Ties* U.S., February 27, 2018. Last assessed 4/30/2020 at: https://www.globaltiesus.org/news/exchangematters/1025-black-american-ambassadors-milestones-in-diplomatic-a-exchange-leadership

McLellan, Carlton E. 2015. "America's Ambassadors of African Descent: A brief history." *The Journal of Pan African Studies,* Vol. 8, No. 2, June 2015.

McLellan, Carlton E. 2015. "Celebrating the History of Black Ambassadorial Leadership." *Association for Diplomatic Studies and Training (ADST*). Last accessed 4/30/2020 at: https://adst.org/inside-foggy-bottom/celebrating-the-leadership-of-americas-ambassadors-of-african-descent/

McLellan, Carlton E. 2015. "Americans Black Ambassadors: An Historical Snapshot." *Blackpast.org.* Last accessed 4/30/2020 at:

http://www.blackpast.org/perspectives/america-s-black-ambassadors-historical-snapshot

McLellan, C. E. 2014. "Celebrating the American Ambassador in Black History." Opinion piece in *Afro-American Newspaper*, Issue 122, No. 30, March 1. Originally published electronically on February 26. Last accessed 4/30/2020 at: https://afro.com/celebrating-the-american-ambassador-in-black-history/

Perry, Cynthia Shepard. 1998. *All Things Being Equal: One Woman's Journey*. Houston: Stonecrest International Publisher

Skinner, Elliott. 1992. *African Americans and U.S. Policy Toward Africa* 1850-1924. Washington, D.C.: Howard University Press

About the Author

Dr. Carlton McLellan (Ph.D.), is a senior diplomacy and international affairs professional and researcher. He is the Founding Director of The American Ambassadors Project and a Senior Fellow with the Association of Black American Ambassadors (ABAA). Dr. McLellan's long-time research interest in Black contributions to diplomacy and foreign affairs led to his founding The American Ambassadors Project, which is the first comprehensive attempt to compile, organize, and report on the lives and contributions of Black Americans who have held the title and rank of U.S. Ambassador. In his 25+ year career in addition to his current work, he has also held research fellowships at educational institutions in South Africa and at the Association of Diplomatic Studies & Training (ADST); worked or consulted at nonprofit, citizen diplomacy-focused agencies such as FHI 360, Global Ties U.S., the Academy for Educational Development (AED), the Institute of International Education (IIE), Meridian International Center, and WorldChicago, all managing U.S. Department of State public diplomacy programs; and at multilateral agencies such as the International Labour Organization (ILO) and the World Bank.

www.ingramcontent.com/pod-product-compliance
Lightning Source LLC
LaVergne TN
LVHW010556110826
845149LV00003B/674

9781967282890